THE COMPLETE ENCYCLOPEDIA OF
CRAFTS

© Marshall Cavendish Limited, 1975
Distributed by Columbia House, 51 West 52nd Street, New York, New York 10019
Printed in U. S. A.

COLUMBIA HOUSE/New York

Contents

Front Cover Photograph: Steve Bicknell
Back Cover Photograph: Peter Dorp

＊ **Not suitable for children without adult supervision**

ADDRESSES
OF MAIL
ORDER SUPPLIERS

ARTS & CRAFTS, GENERAL
California
Gemex Co.
900 W. Los Vallecitos Boulevard
San Marcos, California 92069

Illinois
Lee Wards
Creative Crafts Center
1200 St. Charles Street
Elgin, Illinois 60120

Triarco Arts & Crafts
P. O. Box 106
Northfield, Illinois 60093

Massachusetts
Earth Guild
15 Tudor Street
Cambridge, Massachusetts 02139

Missouri
Skil-Crafts
305 Virginia Avenue
Joplin, Missouri 64801

Nebraska
Mangelsen's
8200 J Street
Omaha, Nebraska 68127

New York
Arthur Brown
2 West 46th Street
New York, New York 10036

Craft Service
337 University Avenue
Rochester, New York 14607

Economy Handicrafts, Inc.
50-21 69th Street
Woodside, N.Y. 11377

Texas
American Handicrafts
P. O. Box 791
Fort Worth, Texas 76101

Wisconsin
Sax Arts and Crafts
207 N. Milwaukee St.
Milwaukee, Wisconsin 53202

BASKETRY
Connecticut
H. H. Perkins
10 S. Bradley Road
Woodbridge, Connecticut 06525

Illinois
Dick Blick Co.
P. O. Box 1267
Galesburg, Illinois 61401

New York
Ace Rattan Products
60-19 54th Place
Maspeth, New York 11378

BATIK
Michigan
Polyproducts Corp.
13810 Nelson Avenue
Detroit, Michigan 48227

New York
Utrecht Linens
33 35th Street
Brooklyn, New York 11232

BEADS
California
The Bead Game
8071 Beverly Boulevard
Los Angeles, California 90048

New York
Grey Owl Indian Mfg. Co., Inc.
150-02 Beaver Road
Jamaica, New York 11433

South Dakota
Del Trading Post
P. O. Box 248
Mission, South Dakota 57555

BOTTLE-CUTTING
New York
Avalon Industries, Inc.
200 Fifth Avenue
New York, New York 10010

CANDLE-MAKING
California
Gemex Co.
900 West Los Vallecitos Boulevard
San Marcos, California 92069

General Supplies Co.
526 Aviation Road
Fallbrook, California 92028

Sippewisset Wax Works
Box 453
Seaside, California 93955

Florida
Island Crafts
5735 14th Street W.
Bradenton, Florida 33507

Illinois
Triarco Arts & Crafts
P. O. Box 106
Northfield, Illinois 60093

Massachusetts
International Candle House
349 Congress Street
Boston, Massachusetts 02210

K.R. Ruckstuhl, Inc.
P. O. Box 663
Provincetown, Massachusetts 02657

Missouri
Skil-Crafts
305 Virginia Avenue
Joplin, Missouri 64801

Nebraska
Mangelsen's
8200 J Street
Omaha, Nebraska 68127

New Jersey
A. I. Root
1106 East Grand Street
Elizabeth, New Jersey 07201

New York
Economy Handicrafts, Inc.
50-21 69th Street
Woodside, N.Y. 11377

Pennsylvania
George Arold
P. O. Box 99
Hatfield, Pennsylvania 19440

Texas
American Handicrafts
P. O. Box 791
Fort Worth, Texas 76101

Washington
Barker Enterprises
15106—10th Avenue S. W.
Seattle, Washington 98166

Pourette Mfg. Co.
6818 Roosevelt Way, N. E.
Seattle, Washington 98115

Wisconsin
Sax Arts and Crafts
207 N. Milwaukee St.
Milwaukee, Wisconsin 53202

CANING AND RUSHING
California
The Caning Shop
1279 Gilman Street
Berkeley, California 94704

Naturalcraft
2199 Bancroft Way
Berkeley, California 94704

Connecticut
H. H. Perkins
10 S. Bradley Road
Woodbridge, Connecticut 06525

Illinois
Dick Blick Co.
P. O. Box 1267
Galesburg, Illinois 61401

New York
Alnap Co., Inc.
66 Reade Street
New York, New York 10007

CERAMICS MATERIALS AND CLAY
Indiana
American Art Clay Co., Inc.
4717 West 16th Street
Indianapolis, Indiana 46222

ADDRESSES OF MAIL ORDER SUPPLIERS

New York
Long Island Ceramic Center
1190 Route 109
Lindenhurst, New York 11757

DECOUPAGE
Illinois
Dick Blick
P. O. Box 1267
Galesburg, Illinois 61401

Missouri
Skil-Crafts
305 Virginia Avenue
Joplin, Missouri 64801

New York
Economy Handicrafts, Inc.
50-21 69th Street
Woodside, N.Y. 11377

Texas
American Handicrafts
P. O. Box 791
Fort Worth, Texas 76101

DYES
Alabama
Owl and Olive Weavers
704 29th Street South
Birmingham, Alabama 35233

California
The Mercantile
P. O. Box 343
Berkeley, California 94701

Kansas
The Yarn Barn
Box 334
730 Massachusetts
Lawrence, Kansas 66044

Massachusetts
Earth Guild/Grateful Union
15 Tudor Street
Cambridge, Massachusetts 02139

Minnesota
The Yarnery
1648 Grand Avenue
St. Paul, Minnesota 55105

New Mexico
Village Wools Fibercraft Materials
    and Supplies
308 San Felipe, N. W.
Albuquerque, New Mexico 87104

Oregon
Wildflower Fibers
211 N. W. Davis Street
Portland, Oregon 97209

Pennsylvania
Lenos Handcrafts
2037 Walnut Street
Philadelphia, Pennsylvania 19103

Texas
Craft Industries
1513 West Alabama
Houston, Texas 77006

Utah
Intertwine
217 Trolley Square
Salt Lake City, Utah 84102

ENAMELS AND ENAMELLING MATERIALS
California
Seaire
17909 South Hobart Boulevard
Gardena, California 90248

Illinois
Thomas C. Thompson Co.
Highland Park, Illinois 60035

Missouri
Skil-Crafts
305 Virginia Avenue
Joplin, Missouri 64801

New York
Allcraft Tool & Supply Co.
215 Park Avenue
Hicksville, New York 11801

Economy Handicrafts, Inc.
50-21 69th Street
Woodside, N.Y. 11377

Texas
American Handicrafts
P. O. Box 791
Fort Worth, Texas 76101

FLOWER-MAKING MATERIALS
New York
S. Beckenstein, Inc.
130 Orchard Street
New York, New York 10022

GLASS (STAINED)
Arizona
Art Glass of Arizona, Inc.
2047 North 16th Street
Phoenix, Arizona 85006

California
Augustine Glass Works
929-B Pico Boulevard
Santa Monica, California 90405

Glass by Humber
700 Filbert Street
San Francisco, California 94133

Nervo Art Stained Glass Works
4911 Telegraph Avenue
Oakland, California 94609

Illinois
Acme Glass Co.
2215 West Roosevelt Road
Chicago, Illinois 60608

Maryland
CCM Arts and Crafts, Inc.
9520 Baltimore Avenue
College Park, Maryland 20740

Massachusetts
Stained Glass of Hanover
Box 3065
Hanover, Massachusetts 02339

Whittemore-Durgin Glass Co.
Box 2065 AB
Hanover, Massachusetts 02339

Whittemore-Durgin Glass Co.
825 Market Street
Rockland, Massachusetts 02370

New Jersey
Glass Work Bench
159 Main Street
Flemington, New Jersey 08822

Stancraft
2005 Highway 35
Oakhurst, New Jersey 07755

New York
Allcraft Tool & Supply Co.
215 Park Avenue
Hicksville, New York 11801

S. A. Bendheim Co., Inc.
122 Hudson Street
New York, New York 10013

Economy Handicrafts, Inc.
50-21 69th Street
Woodside, N.Y. 11377

Glass Masters Guild
52 Carmine Street
New York, New York 10014

Ohio
Franklin Art Glass Studios
222 East Sycamore Street
Columbus, Ohio 43206

Pennsylvania
Willet Stained Glass Studios
10 E. Moreland Avenue
Philadelphia, Pennsylvania 19118

Texas
American Handicrafts
P. O. Box 791
Fort Worth, Texas 76101

Virginia
Arts & Crafts Studio
7221 Little River Turnpike
Annandale, Virginia 22003

Washington
Alpha Faceting Supply
Box 2133, Dept. C
Bremerton, Washington 98310

Stained Glass Studio
12519 Lake City Way N. E.
Seattle, Washington 98125

ADDRESSES OF MAIL ORDER SUPPLIERS

JEWELRY FINDINGS AND MATERIALS

California

California Crafts Supply
1419 North Central Park Avenue
Anaheim, California 92802

Gemex Co.
900 W. Los Vallecitos Blvd.
San Marcos, California 92069

Jewelart, Inc.
7753 Densmore Avenue
Van Nuys, California 91406

Illinois

Dick Blick
P. O. Box 1267
Galesburg, Illinois 61401

Triarco Arts & Crafts
P. O. Box 106
Northfield, Illinois 60093

Maryland

CCM Arts and Crafts, Inc.
9520 Baltimore Avenue
College Park, Maryland 20740

Michigan

C. R. Hill Co.
35 W. Grand River Avenue
Detroit, Michigan 48226

New York

Allcraft Tool & Supply Co., Inc.
22 West 48th Street
New York, New York 10020

Economy Handicrafts, Inc.
50-21 69th Street
Woodside, N.Y. 11377

Magic Novelty Co., Inc.
95 Morton Street
New York, New York 10014

Vanguard Crafts Inc.
2915 Avenue J
Brooklyn, N.Y. 11210

Ohio

Kraft Korner
5864 Mayfield Road
Cleveland, Ohio 44124

National Artcrafts Supply Co.
12217 Euclid Avenue
Cleveland, Ohio 44160

Wisconsin

Nasco House of Crafts
901 Janesville Avenue
Ft. Atkinson, Wisconsin 53538

Sax Arts and Crafts
207 N. Milwaukee Street
Milwaukee, Wisconsin 53202

KNOTTING AND WEAVING

New Jersey

Boin Arts and Crafts
91 Morris Street
Morristown, New Jersey 07960

New York

P. C. Herwig Co., Inc.
264 Clinton Street
Brooklyn, New York 11201

LEATHERCRAFT

California

California Crafts Supply
1096 North Main Street
Orange, California 92667

Connecticut

S & S Art and Crafts
Colchester, Connecticut 06415

Illinois

Triarco Arts & Crafts
P. O. Box 106
Northfield, Illinois 60093

Massachusetts

Berman Leather
147 S Street
Boston, Massachusetts 02111

Missouri

The Brown Leather Co.
305 Virginia Avenue
Joplin, Missouri 64801

Skil-Crafts
305 Virginia Avenue
Joplin, Missouri 64801

New York

Art Handicrafts Co.
3512 Flatlands Avenue
Brooklyn, New York 11234

Economy Handicrafts, Inc.
50-21 69th Street
Woodside, N.Y. 11377

P. C. Herwig Co., Inc.
264 Clinton Street
Brooklyn, New York 11201

Leathercrafters Supply Co.
25 Great Jones Street
New York, New York 10012

Tandy Leather Co.
330 Fifth Avenue
New York, New York 10018

Wisconsin

Sax Arts and Crafts
207 North Milwaukee Street
Milwaukee, Wisconsin 53202

METALCRAFTING

Illinois

Apollo Metals, Inc.
6650 Oak Park Avenue
Chicago, Illinois 60638

Maryland

CCM Arts and Crafts, Inc.
9520 Baltimore Avenue
College Park, Maryland 20740

New York

Allcraft Tool & Supply Co.
215 Park Avenue
Hicksville, New York 11801

MOSAICS

Illinois

Dick Blick
P. O. Box 1267
Galesburg, Illinois 61401

New York

Economy Handicrafts, Inc.
50-21 69th Street
Woodside, N.Y. 11377

Soriano Ceramics
2021 Steinway Street
Long Island City, New York 11106

NEEDLECRAFTS

California

Gemex Co.
900 W. Los Vallecitos Boulevard
San Marcos, California 92069

Naturalcraft
2199 Bancroft Way
Berkeley, California 94704

Illinois

Lee Wards
1200 St. Charles Street
Elgin, Illinois 60120

New York

Bell Yarn
75 Essex Street
New York, New York 10002

Economy Handicrafts, Inc.
50-21 69th Street
Woodside, N.Y. 11377

Goldman's Yarn Stores, Inc.
4417 13th Avenue
Brooklyn, New York 11219

Alice Maynard
724 Fifth Avenue
New York, New York 10019

Texas

Merribee Needlecraft Co.
2904 W. Lancaster
Ft. Worth, Texas 76107

PAPERCRAFTS AND PAPIER-MÂCHÉ

Connecticut

S & S Art and Crafts
Colchester, Connecticut 06415

Illinois

Dick Blick
P. O. Box 1267
Galesburg, Illinois 61401

ADDRESSES
OF MAIL
ORDER SUPPLIERS

Triarco Arts & Crafts
P. O. Box 106
Northfield, Illinois 60093

Maryland
CCM Arts & Crafts, Inc.
9520 Baltimore Avenue
College Park, Maryland 20740

Missouri
Skil-Crafts
305 Virginia Avenue
Joplin, Missouri 64801

New York
Economy Handicrafts, Inc.
50-21 69th Street
Woodside, N.Y. 11377

Wisconsin
Nasco House of Crafts
901 Janesville Avenue
Ft. Atkinson, Wisconsin 53538

Sax Arts and Crafts
207 N. Milwaukee Street
Milwaukee, Wisconsin 53202

PLASTICS
California
Cadillac Plastic & Chemical Co.
11255 Vanowen
North Hollywood, California 91605

Georgia
Cadillac Plastic & Chemical Co.
1500 Carroll Drive, N. W.
Atlanta, Georgia 30318

Illinois
Cadillac Plastic & Chemical Co.
1245 West Fulton
Chicago, Illinois 60607

Maine
Soule Glass and Paint Co.
127 Marginal Way
Portland, Maine 04101

Maryland
CCM Arts & Crafts, Inc.
9520 Baltimore Avenue
College Park, Maryland 20740

Massachusetts
Cadillac Plastic & Chemical Co.
269 McGarth Highway
Boston, Massachusetts 02143

Michigan
Cadillac Plastic & Chemical Co.
15111 Second Avenue
Detroit, Michigan 48203

Polyproducts Corp.
13810 Nelson Avenue
Detroit, Michigan 48227

New Jersey
Cadillac Plastic & Chemical Co.
6025 Colonial Highway
Pennsauken, New Jersey 08109

Smooth-On Corp.
1000 Valley Road
Gillette, New Jersey 07933

New York
Cadillac Plastic & Chemical Co.
35-21 Vernon Boulevard
Long Island City, New York 11106

Industrial Plastic
309 Canal Street
New York, New York 10013

The Plastics Factory
119 Avenue D
New York, New York 10009

Ohio
Cadillac Plastic & Chemical Co.
3818 Red Bank Road
Cincinnati, Ohio 45227

Texas
Cadillac Plastic & Chemical Co.
2546 Irving Boulevard
Dallas, Texas 75207

ROCK POLISHING
California
Great Western Equipment Co.
3444 Main Street
Chula Vista, California 92011

New Jersey
Craftools Inc.
1 Industrial Road
Wood Ridge, New Jersey 07075

Ohio
National Artcraft Supply Co.
12217 Euclid Avenue
Cleveland, Ohio 44160

Wisconsin
Sax Arts and Crafts
207 N. Milwaukee Street
Milwaukee, Wisconsin 53202

SILKSCREEN
New York
Arthur Brown, Inc.
2 West 46th Street
New York, New York 10036

STONE GRINDING
California
Felker Manufacturing Co.
1900-F So. Crenshaw Boulevard
Torrance, California 90501

Walter E. Johansen
P. O. Box 907
Morgan Hill, California 95037

Indiana
Gemstone Shop
17561 State Road 23 N. E.
South Bend, Indiana 46635

Texas
Gem Center, U.S.A.
4100 Alameda
El Paso, Texas 79905

WIRECRAFTING
Illinois
Dick Blick
P. O. Box 1267
Galesburg, Illinois 61401

Maryland
CCM Arts & Crafts, Inc.
9520 Baltimore Avenue
College Park, Maryland 20740

Missouri
Skil-Crafts
305 Virginia Avenue
Joplin, Missouri 64801

New York
Allcraft Tool and Supply Co.
215 Park Avenue
Hicksville, New York 11801

Economy Handicrafts, Inc.
50-21 69th Street
Woodside, N.Y. 11377

WOODFINDINGS
Maine
Saunders Brothers
Westbrook, Maine 04092

New York
Duplex Novelty Co.
315 West 35th Street
New York, New York 10001

YARN
California
The Yarn Depot, Inc.
545 Sutter Street
San Francisco, California 94102

Connecticut
Cottage Crafts
Pomfret Center, Connecticut 06259

Minnesota
The Yarnery
1648 Grand Avenue
St. Paul, Minnesota 55105

New York
Economy Handicrafts, Inc.
50-21 69th Street
Woodside, N.Y. 11377

Home Yarn Co.
1849 Coney Island Avenue
Brooklyn, New York 11230

Paternayan Bros., Inc.
312 E. 95 Street
New York, New York 10028

Ohio
Colonial Woolen Mills, Inc.
6501 Barberton Avenue
Cleveland, Ohio 44102

Oregon
Oregon Worsted Co.
8300 S. E. McLaughlin Boulevard
Portland, Oregon 97202

Pennsylvania
Walter McCook & Son, Inc.
31 No. 10th Street
Philadelphia, Pennsylvania 19107

Creative ideas 16

Fold and dye paper

Here is an original way to make decorated tissue paper which can be used as delicate wrappings for gifts or as covers for diaries and boxes.

You will need:

Soft, absorbent, white tissue paper.

Any plain white paper.

Paper towels.

Felt pens. These must not be waterproof and the best to use are painting sticks.

Fold the tissue in one of the ways shown (fig.1). Then

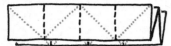

thoroughly wet it and blot between paper towels. Place on a piece of white paper.

Draw design on the top layer with a dotting action —this method deposits more ink, and lines may tear the fine tissue.

Cover wad with white paper and press down on the paper. Separate the folds to check the ink penetration. Go over the design at places where the ink is faint.

As you open the wad to draw on the lower layers the design on the top layers will print onto the white paper, so be sure to keep the wad in the same position on the backing paper or the design will smudge.

After you have finished the drawing, leave the wad for a few minutes to allow the ink to penetrate completely. With small pieces of tissue you can unfold the paper and leave it open to dry on white paper. If the tissue is large, partially unfold it and place layers of clean paper in between.

With a cool iron press until almost dry. Unfold, place again between clean papers and iron out flat.

If used for gift wrapping, first wrap the gift in white paper to give emphasis to the clear ink colors.

If you want to cover books or boxes use a spray-on adhesive, sparingly.

Melvin Grey

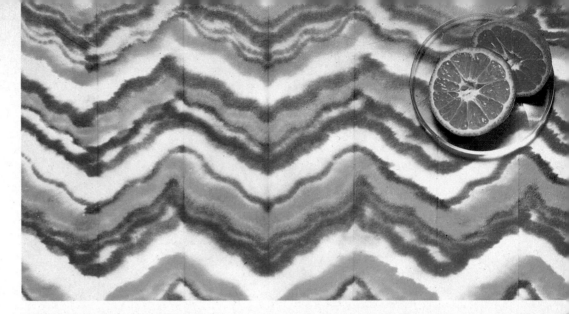

449

Cutting and gluing

Glass 4

Glass can be cut quite simply and with a little practice you will be able to cut lines and curves in plain or stained glass to make shapes to your own design which can be stuck together to form windows, panels or screens.

In this chapter a stained glass window is made by cutting and gluing. (Methods of leading are left to a later chapter.) Plain glass can be used and then painted with transparent glass paints as described in Glass chapter 3, page 366. Alternatively, use traditional stained glass. This may be very expensive so try the glass paints first. In both cases a backing sheet of clear glass provides support.

The sun window
Tools
Glass cutter. Use a steel wheel glass cutter.

Radius glass cutter. A cutting wheel mounted on an adjustable arm which revolves on a central pivot fastened to a suction cap. The radius cutter is not absolutely necessary though it is useful for cutting circles.

Pliers.

Wallpaper roller or rolling pin.

Goggles.

Materials
Two sheets of glass about 3mm ($\frac{1}{10}$") thick, bought from a glass dealer, one sheet to be cut up and painted, the other sheet to be used for backing. If you are using real stained glass buy several smaller sheets in amber, blue, yellow and green.

Transparent glass paint, if you are starting with plain glass and then painting it. There are several kinds of suitable paints available which can be bought either in the form of a kit or on their own.

Epoxy glue to stick one piece of glass to another.

'Leading', the resin kind which comes in two parts and is mixed together to form a long roll. This leading is not essential but it does make the design stand out and gives it a more 'finished' look. Leading sometimes comes as part of a glass staining kit.

Silicon carbide paper, the fine wet and dry variety, for smoothing rough edges.

Denatured alcohol for cleaning glass.

Light machine oil, such as sewing machine oil, for lubricating the cutting wheel.

Turpentine for cleaning brushes.

Sheet of cardboard the same size or bigger than the glass.

Lampblack.

This decorative plant holder can easily be made using cutting and sticking techniques. A plain piece of glass is cut to shape, color painted and leaded as described in this chapter, and glued on to an ordinary metal shelf bracket. Using bottle cutting equipment (Glass chapter 2, page 254) a green bottle is cut to make a plant holder. Supplied by Craft Materials Supplies.

Right: the finished window, simple but effective. It can either be made with traditional stained glass or using transparent glass paints.

Designed by Anthony Wilson.

Steve Bicknell

Melvin Grey

Plain white paper the same size as the glass.
Masking tape, ruler, felt-tipped pen or wax crayon.

Method

Draw the design onto a piece of paper the same size as the sheet of glass. Keep the design simple with not too many intricate curves or sharp corners. Not only are they difficult to cut but stress points at corners could shatter the glass. Keep the sections of the design on the large side because larger pieces of glass are easier to cut than smaller pieces.

Cutting. Lay the design on a flat surface which is covered with a piece of protective cardboard. Place the glass over the design and tape the top corners to keep it firm (fig.1).

*Victoria Drew*

1. *Tape the glass over the design, clean with denatured alcohol, and mark the lines of the design on the glass. Cut the bottom section first.*

If real stained glass is being used, each segment of color is cut one at a time. It may help to draw the design onto stiff cardboard, then cut it up into sections to make a set of templates or patterns with a separate template for each section of the design. Draw each section separately. If using templates be sure to cut just inside the line.

Before starting work on the glass clean off any dirt and grease with denatured alcohol. Then mark the lines of the design on the glass with crayon.

Start cutting bottom sections first.

Lubricate the glass cutter beforehand by wiping it with a piece of felt which has been soaked in light machine oil. Hold the cutter so that the handle rests between the first and second fingers and thumb, and the bottom of the hand remains clear of the glass.

Score the surface of the glass along the line with the cutter. Draw the cutter toward you, keeping the action smooth. Don't press too hard, or backtrack because the glass may break at a point where you do not intend it to. The scoring should be completed in one operation, the object being to score the surface of the glass evenly so that the piece can be easily tapped apart. Once the score mark is made, turn the glass over and lightly tap it with the end of the glass cutter along the silvery score line. Keep the glass flat on the table. It will start splitting but keep on tapping until the two pieces separate. Patience and a light hand are essential at this stage.

If you are making a design with small strips or pieces of glass score the line as before and then, wearing goggles and using the jaws of a pair of pliers, break off the glass in small pieces.

Cutting circles. A radius cutter is the special tool needed for cutting circles or semi-circles, but you can make a perfectly satisfactory circle by using an ordinary glass cutter fastened to a length of string. The other end of the

Hold the glass cutter firmly but lightly and score the surface of the glass by drawing the cutter toward you.

string is held down in the center of the circle.

If you are cutting glass for the first time it is a good idea to practice on some waste pieces of glass first—just to get the feel of the cutter.

Smoothing rough edges. When all the sections are cut, rub the edges with wet silicon carbide paper. Don't overdo the smoothing because the pieces may then not fit back together. On the other hand, allowance should be made for the glue you use to take up a small amount of space between the edges.

Painting. If you have been using a sheet of plain glass the different parts of the design will need to be color varnished. Load a fairly coarse brush with paint and drop onto the glass, working from edge to edge. Do not brush the paint too much because it tends to spread out on its own and find its own density. Paint on the reverse side of the design and leave the paint to dry overnight in a dust-free room—if the atmosphere is dirty bits and pieces will adhere to the glass.

Gluing. When all the sections are varnished and dried they can be stuck to the backing sheet of glass. Starting at the bottom, put a little glue along the cut edges of the first piece and place it in position (fig.2). There is no need to glue the whole flat surface of the glass. The glue from the edges will spread out underneath the cut sections to hold them in place.

Dick Miller

A radius cutter is the right tool for cutting circles. Hold the center steady and swing around the cutting arm.

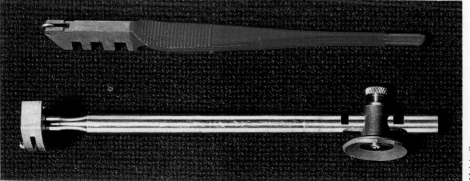

Melvin Grey

Glass wheel cutter and the radius cutter. Supplied by Craft Materials Supplies.

2. *Glue cut pieces of glass onto backing sheet with a little glue squeezed along the edges of each piece.*

Make sure when sticking the glass that the varnished side is placed down in contact with the backing sheet. This will have the effect of protecting the varnish and of adding extra translucency to the color. Stained glass is often smooth only on one side and this side should be stuck to the plain glass.

Position the other sections in place, coating the edges with just the right amount of glue so that a little squeezes out on the backing glass.

Don't worry if the glue oozes out on to the top of the glass—leave it to dry and then gently scrape off any excess with a sharp knife or blade.

Mock leading. When all the sections are in place and the glue is completely hardened, the 'leading' can be added along the joins. Roll out the leading on a dry wood board and position it along the joins, then roll over with a hard wallpaper roller or rolling pin dipped in water (fig.3). Finally smooth the leading with a moistened finger.

The leading putty takes about three hours to dry; when it is hard rub a damp cloth over it. Fine wire wool can remove any stubborn smears and **raise a luster on the glass.**

Finish off the leading with a soft cloth dipped in lampblack and finally buff it with a duster.

How to use the window

The window is now ready and can be put into a window frame in the usual way or left free-standing.

Alternatively, glue wire around the edges of the glass (using epoxy glue) or attach to the glass with the 'leading'. Leave a loop at the top of the glass and hang in front of your window or other source of light.

Steve Bicknell

This lampshade can be made from a large bottle, and decorated. Supplied by Craft Materials Supplies.

3. *Roll out leading into a long, thin strip and apply along the glued edges of design for a complete finish.*

Cutting the lampshade

An attractive lampshade can be made quite simply from a glass carboy or demijohn bottle.

Draw a line with a felt-tipped pen around the bottle, making sure that it is the same distance from the top all the **way around. Then score the line with the glass cutter in the usual way.**

Tap the cutting line from the inside of the bottle. You may have to improvise a tapper; a small stone tied to the end of a ruler or metal rod would be sufficient. If you have a bottle-cutting kit use the tapper provided (the actual bottle cutter is not suitable for large bottles).

After edges have been rubbed smooth, as described above, paint with glass paints. Apply leading as described in the method given above.

453

Carving and casting in plaster

Plaster of Paris can be cast to make decorative plaques. In this chapter, a very simple, quick project, and one that is more challenging indicate the variety of ways in which you can use this versatile material.

Plaster stamps

Damp clay does not stick to hardened plaster of Paris, so raised designs and insignia made in plaster can be used to stamp a motif on the surface of clay while the clay is still damp and capable of taking a sharp, clear impression. Sometimes a plaster stamp is used to make a series of impressions to create a textural design on a pot or tile.

To make a signature seal

You will need:
A lump of clay or plasticine.
A piece of paper to make a tube to encircle the design comfortably, and about 10cm (4") high.
Plaster of Paris.
Knife or modeling tool.

☐ Work the clay or plasticine into a smooth, square shape and use the knife or modeling tool to carve out an initial, or a simple design that will serve as your 'stamp' for your own pots. For example, you might try a stylized bird, a five-petaled flower, or a star.

☐ Remember that if you want the seal to be the motif and no more, it is sufficient to carve it direct onto the surface of the modeling material (fig.1). If, however, you would like to have a 'frame', first carve out a suitable shape and then carve the motif at a second, deeper level (fig.1).

☐ Surround the completed design with a paper tube, pressing the end of the tube firmly into the modeling material so that the liquid plaster of Paris cannot dribble out (fig.2).

1. *Carve the motif directly for a simple signature, at a deeper level for a 'frame'.*

2. *Surround the carving with a paper tube, pressing it firmly against the clay.*

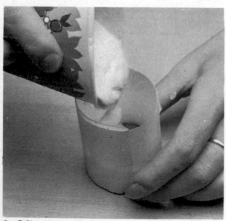

3. *Mix a small amount of plaster of Paris to the right consistency and carefully pour out the liquid plaster to almost fill the paper tube.*

4. *Below: look for interesting objects to create delicate stamp designs.*

Iain Reid

454

☐ Mix the plaster of Paris, and carefully pour it to almost fill the paper tube (fig.3).

☐ Leave to dry out thoroughly, preferably overnight.

☐ Remove the clay or plasticine from the end of the tube, tear away the paper and the stamp is ready for use.

Interesting objects such as carved buttons, signet rings, brooches or badges could also be used to make the original impression (fig.4). Stamps made in this way are often particularly delicate in outline and they can be used to produce fine, regular detailing around the rim of a pot or the edge of a small tile.

To carve a stamp design

Large, bold designs can be made by carving a motif directly on to the plaster stamp.

You will need:

Paper drinking cup.

Plaster of Paris.

Old knife or wood-carving tool.

☐ Mix the plaster and pour it into the paper cup.

It is a good idea to make several plaster blocks at one time so that you can experiment with a variety of carved designs from finely etched line patterns to large, chunky shapes.

☐ Leave until it is just hard, and then tear off the paper.

☐ Use a pencil or a pin to roughly sketch a design on the smaller end of the plaster block.

It becomes more difficult to carve plaster as it hardens more thoroughly, so it is a good idea to do the bulk of the carving at once (fig.5).

☐ Then leave the stamp for a few hours or overnight. Finish off any fine detailing or cleaning of the design when the plaster is quite hard.

☐ As you carve, test the design on a slab of damp clay from time to time to check the effect that you are aiming for.

Stamps for decoration

Different stamp designs can be very effective if they are grouped together on one piece. Try rolling out a square slab of clay about 2.5cm (1″) deep. Impress it with each of the carved designs, at random or grouped in rows. After the clay has been fired, a piece made like this could make an interesting table or sideboard stand for hot dishes and plates (fig.6).

5. *Carve the main bulk of the design before the plaster dries out thoroughly.*

6. *A group of designs impressed on a clay slab makes an interesting trivet. Right: finer designs can be traced and carved with the point of a pin.*

Joy Simpson

Lace and wheel motifs

The previous crochet chapters explained how to make flat granny square motifs and circular motifs. These versatile motifs can be adapted to any size, either by means of additional chain spaces or by continuously increasing the number of stitches in each round. These motifs have to be joined together after completion by means of a sewn overcasting seam, or by crocheting them together, through both thickness-

Melvin Grey

es, using an ordinary single crochet stitch.

This chapter deals with square lace and Catherine-wheel motifs which can be joined to each subsequent motif as part of the last round, thus avoiding any seaming. However, if you want to work them singly they can be sewn together by catching each loop where it touches the corresponding loop of the next motif.

With all these motifs the exciting thing to remember is that they provide unlimited scope for original designs to suit your own taste and requirements. You will find a few suggestions for yarns and ways of using these motifs here.

See how many original ideas you can attempt, starting with something simple like pillow covers, bedspreads, shawls and tabards.

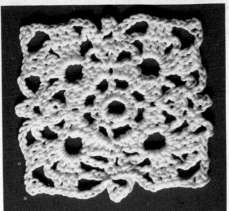

Detail of square lace motif used for place mat and coaster shown opposite.

The simple stitches you have learned can be used for all sorts of motifs, including these two completely different lacy ones. The motifs can be worked in fine or thick yarns, depending on purpose or personal choice.

A thicker cotton yarn will produce a much larger motif which can form the basis of a superb bedspread—lightweight woolen yarn could be used for a lacy evening shawl.

Square lace motif

Make 6ch. Join with sl st to first ch to form circle.

1st round. 2ch to count as first sc, work 15sc into circle. Join with sl/st to second of first 2ch. (For single crochet and half double crochet see Crochet chapter 2, page 94.)

2nd round. 4ch to count as first hdc and 2ch, *skip 1sc, 1hdc into next sc, 2ch, rep from * 6 times more. Join with sl/st to second of first 4ch.

3rd round. Work (1sc, 1hdc, 1dc, 1hdc, 1sc, 1ch) into each ch sp to end. Join with sl/st to first sc. 8 petals.

4th round. 2ch to count as first hdc *3ch, 1sc into dc of next petal, 4ch, 1sc into dc of next petal, 3ch, 1hdc into 1ch sp before next petal, 2ch, 1hdc into same ch sp, rep from * twice more, 3ch 1sc into dc of next petal, 4ch, 1sc into dc of next petal, 3ch, 1hdc into last 1ch sp after last petal, 2ch. Join with sl/st to second of first 2ch.

5th round. 1ch, *4ch, into 4ch sp work (3dc, 3ch, 3dc) to form corner, 4ch, 1sc into hdc, 1sc into 2ch sp, 1sc into hdc, rep from * twice more, 4ch, into 4ch sp work (3dc, 3ch, 3dc), 4ch, 1sc into hdc, 1sc into 2ch sp. Join with sl/st to first ch.

6th round. 1ch, *5ch, 1dc into each of next 3dc, 5ch, insert hook into third ch from hook to form a little loop (fig.1),

1. *Forming a picot loop by inserting hook into the third chain from hook.*

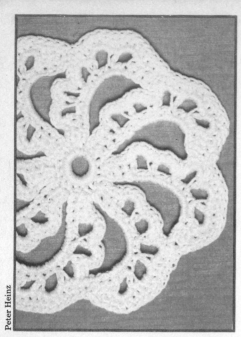

Peter Heinz

Catherine-wheel motif with eight spokes.

and work 1sc to form picot—called 5ch picot—2ch, 1dc into each of next 3dc, 5ch, sl/st into next sc, 4ch, insert hook into third ch from hook and work 1sc to form picot—called 4ch picot—1ch, skip 1sc, sl/st into next sc, rep from * twice more, 5ch, 1dc into each of next 3dc, 5ch picot, 2ch, 1dc into each of next 3dc, 5ch, sl/st into next sc, 4ch picot, 1ch. Join with sl/st to first ch. Fasten off.

To join square lace motifs
Work first 5 rounds as given for square lace motif.
6th round (joining round). 1ch, *5ch, 1dc into each of next 3dc, 2ch, with RS of completed motif A facing RS of motif B which is to be joined work 1sc into 5ch picot at corner of motif A, 2ch, 1dc into each of next 3dc of motif B, sl/st into first of 5ch after last dc on motif A, 4ch, sl/st into next sc of motif B, 1ch, 1sc into 4ch picot of motif A, 1ch, skip 1sc on motif B, sl/st into next sc on motif B, 4ch, sl/st into last ch before next 3dc on motif A, 1dc into each of next 3dc on motif B, 2ch, 1sc into 5ch picot at corner of motif A, 2ch. One side has been joined. Complete round motif B as given for square lace motif A. Fasten off. Where the squares have to be joined on two sides continue in the same way.

Place mat and coaster

Requirements for place mat 28cm (11¼″) wide by 23cm (9″) deep and coaster 11cm (4½″) square. Each motif measures 5.5cm (2¼″) square.
40gm of No.20 cotton. 1 ball makes approximately 23 motifs.
One No.1.50 ISR (US size A) crochet hook.
Place mat
Work as given for square lace motif,

joining 5 motifs to form one row, 4 rows in all, total 20 motifs.
Coaster
Work as given for square lace motif, joining 2 motifs to form one row, 2 rows in all, total 4 motifs.

Catherine wheel motif

Make 8ch. Join with sl/st to first ch to form circle.
1st round. 1ch to count as first sc, work 15sc into circle. Join with sl/st to first ch. 16 sts. Do not break off yarn.
First spoke of Catherine-wheel
1st row. Make 14ch, work 1sc into third ch from hook, 1sc into next ch, work 10sc around, and not into, the ch, 1sc into each of last 3ch, sl/st into next sc along the circle, turn.
2nd row. Work 1sc into each of first

11 10 9 7 5 3 5 7 9 10 11

Diagram to show how a café curtain is formed from strips of Catherine-wheel motifs.

3sc, (4ch, skip 1sc, 1sc into next sc) 5 times, 1sc into each of next 2sc, 1sc into second of first 2ch. Turn.
3rd row. 1ch to count as first sc, 1sc into each of next 3sc, (4sc into 4ch loop, 1sc into next sc) 5 times, 1sc into each of last 2sc, sl/st into next sc along the circle, turn.
Second spoke of Catherine-wheel
1st row. Make 13ch, sl/st into center st of third loop along first spoke, turn, work 1sc into each of next 3ch, work 10sc around the ch, 1sc into each of last 3ch, sl/st into next sc along circle, turn and complete as for first spoke but on next row end with 1sc into each of last 3sc instead of last 2sc and turning ch.
Work 6 more spokes in the same way and when working the last one, join the center of the 3rd loop to the tip of the first spoke. Fasten off. Total 8 spokes.
Last round. Rejoin yarn with sl/st to top of any spoke, 1ch to count as first sc, work 1sc into each st around outside

edge of motif. Join with sl/st to first ch. Fasten off.

Café curtain

For curtain 140cm (55″) wide by 140cm (55″) long, excluding tabs. Each motif measures 13cm (5″) diameter.
You will need:
11 x 84m (77yd) balls of 4 ply cotton thread in main shade, A, 10 balls of contrast color, B, 9 balls of contrast color, C and 7 balls each of contrast colors, D and E. 1 ball makes 2 motifs. One No.3.00 ISR (US size F) crochet hook.
Length of wooden curtain rail.
To make café curtain
Make 22 catherine wheel motifs in A, 20 in B, 18 in C, 14 in D and 13 in E.
To make up
Join motifs tog as shown in diagram.
Tabs. Using No.3.00 ISR (US size F) hook, appropriate color and with RS of first top motif facing, rejoin yarn with sl/st to fifth sc along edge, 3ch to count as first dc, work 1dc into each of next 5sc, turn. 6 sts. Cont working rows of dc across these 6 sts until tab is long enough to go over top of curtain rail and down to top of motif. Fasten off. Work 10 more tabs in same way. St tabs in place to back of each motif.

A beautiful, lacy café curtain is created by joining strips of Catherine wheel motifs together and suspending them from a wooden curtain rail.

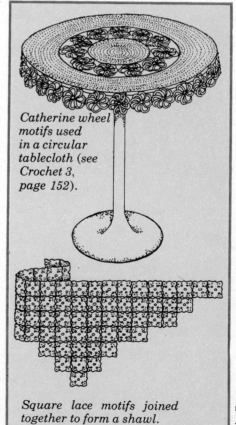

Catherine wheel motifs used in a circular tablecloth (see Crochet 3, page 152).

Square lace motifs joined together to form a shawl.

Lesley Fox
Camera Press

Using wood scraps

Odd bits and scraps of wood which have been left over from other carpentry projects should never be thrown away. Put them in a box or bin near your working area—sooner or later you will find a use for them. You can use them for trying out a drill, for blocks under a C-clamp to protect the wood surface, or as a block or support on which to stand newly painted wood.

You can make even better use of scraps by using them for small projects, such as collages, hangings and toys, that are both fun to do and practical. It's very satisfying to use up everything, whether it's bits of picture frame molding, pieces of dowel or left-over plywood scraps. Many local lumber dealers throw away the scraps that could be yours for the asking, including hardwoods such as mahogany, birch or teak.

Using old chair legs

Sometimes old tables or chairs that are being thrown away can be taken apart and stripped down to reveal old hardwoods that are expensive to buy today. For example, turned and shaped chair or table legs can be sawn off and used for things like attractive candle holders. Just cut off the particular piece you want so that it will stand up, then drill a hole in the top for the candle. Or make egg-cups the same way by cutting the piece shorter and making the top hole larger.

Collages

Perhaps the easiest and most interesting application is in making collages out of scraps of wood. For these, almost any bits of wood can be used, and the more unusual the better.

Simply arrange and glue pieces of wood in interesting patterns onto a backing board such as a piece of hardwood or plywood. It's very easy to adapt the design to suit your pieces. Most pieces, particularly scraps of old picture frames, are attractive when arranged in the right way. You can add texture and interest by sawing grooves in some pieces, cutting holes or chiseling out designs in others.

You don't have to finish it in one day—leave it unfinished and then when you get an idea or the right piece of scrap add it to the collage. Perhaps you could give a touch of color by coloring in the grooves with a felt-tipped pen.

Remember to keep the design fairly simple. It doesn't matter if there are large plain pieces scattered through it —they make the other areas more interesting.

A 3mm ($\frac{1}{8}$") piece of Masonite can be used as a spacer to get a constant width between the various pieces.

Wall hangings

Another dramatic idea for using up bits of wood is to join them together with string and to hang them from a piece of dowel to make a 'tapestry' of wood.

Arrange the wood to the lengths you want them to hang, allowing for the string to join them together. Drill holes to pass the string through and leave some to tie the string around.

The string should be as interesting as possible—old pieces of rope or twine are attractive and also vary the texture. Tie the string to the dowel and attach to the pieces as you have arranged to use them. If you have drilled a hole and want to prevent the wood from slipping

Wood leftovers and bits of scrap plywood can be used to make attractive collages. The pieces are glued to a board. Designed by Cyril Foster.

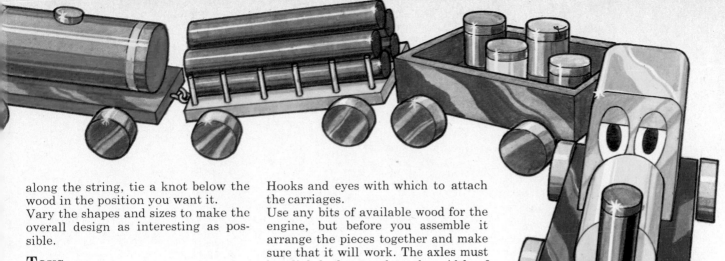
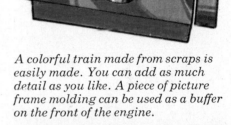

along the string, tie a knot below the wood in the position you want it.

Vary the shapes and sizes to make the overall design as interesting as possible.

Toys

Children's toys make ideal projects because wood not only looks and feels good but is practically indestructible.

Toys today are expensive but if you make them yourself they can be as elementary as an arrangement of wooden blocks of various sizes and shapes. Or they can be a little more involved, such as wooden trains. They are really simple and particularly fun to make and then give away as presents.

To make a train

You will need:

Pieces of dowel in 3 thicknesses, say 6mm (¼″) for the axles, 19mm (¾″) for the chimney and 4cm (1½″) for the boiler tank and wheels.

Plywood or softwood for the base.

Softwood for the undercarriage.

Softwood for the cab.

Wood glue.

Sandpaper (fine grade).

Hooks and eyes with which to attach the carriages.

Use any bits of available wood for the engine, but before you assemble it arrange the pieces together and make sure that it will work. The axles must be slightly longer than the width of the base, plus the width of two wheels to allow the wheels to turn freely (fig.1).

☐ To secure the boiler tank flatten it along its length with a rasp or sandpaper and glue this flat side to the base. You can make it more complicated by adding a piece of picture frame molding for a buffer and bits of wire (or string glued into position) for the water pipes.

☐ Drill the holes in the undercarriage and glue to the base. If you secure each piece in a vice or C-clamp until it is dry, it will strengthen the toy.

☐ The carriages are made in a similar way but, instead of using dowel for a chimney and boiler tank, use strips of wood to make carriages; or use upright pieces of dowel to hold logs together, or a large piece of dowel can be used as a tanker.

Building blocks. The simplest toy of all is the basic wooden block. Some-

A colorful train made from scraps is easily made. You can add as much detail as you like. A piece of picture frame molding can be used as a buffer on the front of the engine.

Paul Williams

Tool box

The tools you use will depend on the wood you have and on each particular project. Usually, the only essential tools are a carpenter's square, tape measure, saw, brace with drill bits, and a Surform or rasp to scrape off corners if necessary.

A Surform has perforations in its surface which allow the shavings to fall away. A rasp is solid and tends to get clogged with shavings if it is used on softwood and should be cleaned with a coarse brush. However, if you have a rasp the results will be just as satisfactory as those of a Surform. Both Surforms and rasps are available in flat or round surfaces.

Use a Surform when you need to remove a large amount of wood and finish with a file or fine grade sandpaper.

In order to use the Surform the wood must be secured by means of a vice or C-clamp. Hold the Surform by the handle with one hand and use the other hand to guide it as you stroke the wood away from you. Always try to work along the grain to avoid splintering the edge.

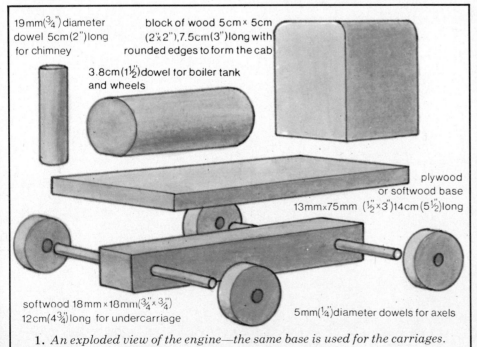

19mm(¾″) diameter dowel 5cm(2″)long for chimney

block of wood 5cm × 5cm (2″×2″),7.5cm(3″)long with rounded edges to form the cab

3.8cm(1½″)dowel for boiler tank and wheels

plywood or softwood base 13mm×75mm (½″×3″)14cm(5½″)long

softwood 18mm×18mm(¾″×¾″) 12cm(4¾″)long for undercarriage

5mm(¼″)diameter dowels for axels

1. An exploded view of the engine—the same base is used for the carriages.

how this often turns out to be the most used of all toys. Any odd bits of wood can be sanded down and made into a toy by adding them to a collection of blocks of various colors, that get constantly stacked up and knocked down. You can also make a box in which to store them (see Carpentry chapter 4, page 236).

You can improve the blocks by sticking or stenciling numbers and letters on them, or by drilling holes through them so that they can be joined together by using dowels.

The Robot

This very simple, ingenious toy will give a child many hours of pleasure. Select pieces of wood that will give the proportions of the robot, ie thicker dowel for the legs than for the arms, and the head at least half the size (or smaller) of the body.

To position the arms drill a hole through the block used for the trunk, slightly larger than the dowel which will pass through it. This will allow the arms to swing freely. Drill holes of the same size through the dowels which will form the arms.

Assemble as illustrated. Glue two pieces of dowel to the bottom of the trunk for the legs.

Glue on a block of wood for the head. The head is not in the center but should be placed slightly toward the back of the robot.

This is a very simple toy to make and if left to dry properly will stand up to some rough handling. It can be varied

and made more flexible by drilling a hole in the bottom of the head and another one in the trunk, and then by using a piece of dowel for the neck, allowing the head to turn around.

Adjustable sculpture

This piece of sculpture will give children and adults a lot of fun; it can be rearranged over and over again or it can be left as in the picture. It can be made in any size. The one illustrated is about 45cm (18") high.

You will need:
Softwood 100mm x 100mm (4"x4"), 12.5cm (5") long, for the base.
Mild steel strip 43cm (17") long, 18mm ($\frac{3}{4}$") wide and about 3mm ($\frac{1}{8}$") thick; aluminum can be used as it is easier to bend.
Wood scraps for the blocks.
General purpose adhesive such as Elmer's Glue-All.
Masking tape.
Rip tape.
Wood primer.
Gloss paint in various colors.

□ Cut the pieces of wood scraps into various sizes and shapes so that you have different sizes ranging from small to large pieces—about 40 pieces in all.
□ Stick a length of masking tape to one surface of each block. This will be the surface placed against the central rod. The larger the block the larger the piece of tape should be.
□ Seal the blocks with wood primer.
□ When dry, paint with various colors of gloss paint.
□ When dry, remove the masking tape.

A toy or a piece of sculpture—it's fun and attractive. Designer R. Polley.

□ Cut pieces of the smoother side of the rip tape to fit the patches left by the masking tape.
Glue the rip tape to the patches.
□ Insert metal strip at one end into a vice and bend it slightly (fig.1).

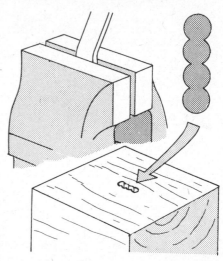

1. The metal strip is placed in the holes; use a wood filler to secure if necessary.

□ In the base block drill a series of holes in a straight line in the center to the width of the metal strip (fig.1).
□ Glue the tape with the coarse surface to the strip, on both sides, leaving the end which fits into the slot free.
□ Insert strip in slot with glue or plug with filler.
□ Arrange the blocks of wood around the strip, putting the tape side to the strip. Play around with the blocks so that the pieces are balanced.

Left: this delightful robot is glued and clamped together to dry, making it very strong. The arms are attached to a piece of dowel which passes through the chest. Designed by Roger Polley.
Right: the sculpture can be re-arranged in many different ways.

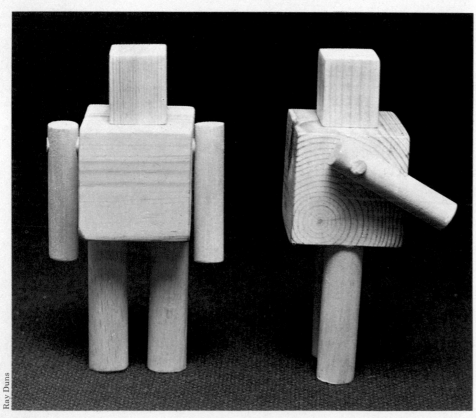

Marbling with seaweed

Color — marbling 2

The art of marbling is enjoying an enthusiastic revival. The variety of the patterns and the vividness of the colors, the fact that almost any surface can be marbled and the sheer fun of doing it make it one of the most agreeable of occupations. Playing with floating marbling colors and teasing them into patterns is a fascinating process and once you start it is easy to get hooked.

There is an increasing demand for marbled goods but, because marbling cannot so far be practiced on a large-scale commercial basis, demand still exceeds supply and if you become proficient you can make it pay.

Various methods of marbling exist. All are based on the principle of floating colors on water (see Marbling chapter 1, page 438). Some methods are faster and easier than others and produce both quick and colorful results, but for the finest control of patterns and the greatest beauty of color a somewhat more complex method is necessary. Briefly, it involves using specially prepared colors from carrageen moss (Irish seaweed).

Seaweed marbling

Seaweed marbling produces colors that are unbelievably bright and vivid and, because the colors can be controlled so well, the patterns are especially easy to form. Any number can be produced and as your experience and confidence grow you will be able to swirl and comb the colors into finely regulated waves or twist them into delicate flower-like motifs.

Paper is the best thing to begin marbling on and marbled papers can be used in a wide variety of ways—as linings for drawers and boxes, coverings on notebooks and wastepaper baskets or to make a patchwork screen.

Lampshades can be cut from manilla paper and marbled to match your decor. You can marble papers for gift wrapping or, if you are more intrepid, you can marble your own wallpaper. Suitably covered and protected marbled paper can also be used on table mats, coffee tables and tray tops.

Equally wonderful effects can be got by marbling directly on to plastics, cloth and leather.

The materials and equipment for seaweed marbling take some effort to prepare but the result is well worth the trouble.

You will need:

Carrageen moss (Irish seaweed).
Formalin (formaldehyde).
Alum (sulphate of aluminum potassium).
Prepared marbling colors.
Oxgall.
Old newspapers.
Tray or trough for marbling.
Small sticks or brushes; eye dropper.
Pots or saucers for paints and one saucepan.
Material for marbling.
Knitting needle for swirling colors.
Fine sieve or old nylon stocking.

Carrageen moss can be obtained at health food shops, wine making suppliers and some drug stores, while alum and formalin, a preservative, are both available at drug stores.

Your tray or trough should be about 61cm x 30.5cm (24"x12") and deep enough to allow size solution to a depth of 2.5cm-5cm (1"-2"). The type of plastic tray used by butchers and bakers is suitable, or a photographic dish which is rather more expensive.

Colors for marbling can be bought specially prepared for this purpose, but if these are difficult to find at your art shop you can use solid poster color pigments. These must be finely ground using a pestle and mortar and then mixed with water.

Preparation

To make the size put 28gm (1oz) of

A galaxy of floating, marbled colors: made by suspending specially prepared paint on an Irish seaweed size, this process makes infinitely subtle patterns. Wall paper is by Caroline Davis.

Melvin Grey

carrageen moss and 1.2lit (2pt) of water in a clean container such as a large saucepan and bring gradually to the boil over a low heat. Allow to boil for 3 or 4 minutes, stirring all the time. It is most important to take special care at this stage because success or failure could depend on it.

☐ Remove mixture from heat and stir in 1.2lit (2pt) of cold water, then 3 dessertspoonful of formalin.

☐ Let the mixture stand for about 12 hours, overnight will do, in a cool place. It should set to form a jelly-like solution.

☐ Strain the size through a fine sieve or old nylon stocking. The formalin acts as a preserving agent and the size, if not used at once, can now be kept for several weeks.

To prepare colors with oxgall. Oxgall is usually obtained ready for use from art supply shops. If necessary, however, you can make your own but it is a slightly messy process. There is no synthetic substitute.

It is best to start by preparing and practicing with only one or two colors, as it takes quite some time using oxgall to balance each color and to get them to spread equally.

Pour 2 teaspoonful of each color into separate jars and initally add 6 drops oxgall to each. Stir thoroughly. Oxgall is added to colors to reduce surface tension and cause them to spread on the surface of the size.

Colors can be dropped on top of each other or side by side. Usually the second color added to the tray needs more oxgall than the first. Try 10 drops, and continue adjusting the proportions until you have achieved the right consistency.

Oxgall is obtainable from a slaughterhouse. Add 1lit (1¾ pt) oxgall to 0.28lit (½pt) denatured alcohol and mix well until the gall has dissolved. Put it in a bottle, seal and leave for about 24 hours so that the fatty sediment can settle to the bottom. Then decant the solution.

Paper. Cut old newspaper into 8cm (3″) strips and the same length as the width of the marbling trough. These will be used to skim the surface between each marbling.

If you are marbling paper, cut each sheet fractionally smaller than the trough. Most papers can be marbled—drawing paper, brown wrapping paper and manilla paper are all suitable.

Mordant. The material to be marbled must be mordanted first. A mordant, in this case alum, is a chemical which makes material and color receptive to one another and improves color tone and colorfastness.

To prepare mordant add 28g (1oz) of alum to 0.57lit (1pt) of hot water. Stir until crystals are dissolved.

Martin Chaffer

Marbled papers were originally used for bookbinding, but they have a number of ingenious and practical uses as the photographs above and opposite show.

Testing

The color and size must always be tested before beginning.

Skim the surface of the size first, then stir the color and drop a speck onto the size with a brush or stick. It should expand evenly to a diameter of 5cm-7.5cm (2″-3″).

If color does not spread, add two or more drops of oxgall, skim the size and test again. If it still does not spread, the size is probably too thick and needs to be thinned with cold water.

If the color spreads and then shrinks, the size is probably colder than the colors and a little warm water should be mixed with the size.

The aim is to get the size to the correct viscosity so that it will hold the pattern after it has been drawn on its surface.

To marble

☐ Mordant material first; sponge the alum solution evenly over the surface to be marbled and for the best results, marble while still damp.

☐ Fill the tray to about 2.5cm (1″) with the marbling size and place it near a sink because you will need running water later on.

☐ Always start by skimming the surface of the size with old newspaper strips. Then stir up each color and drop spots of color over the entire surface leaving enough room for each spot to spread properly.

☐ You are now ready to create your pattern. Using a knitting needle or other pointed instrument, swirl and pattern the colors by dragging it

465

To make a typical combed pattern, float colors as shown.

Draw a knitting needle through the color crosswise.

Then draw the needle lengthwise through colors and finally, to get regulated waves, draw a comb across as shown below.

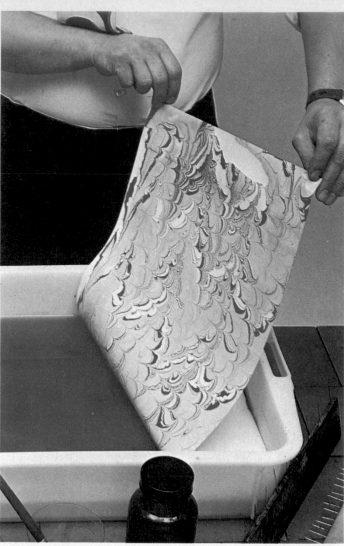

To print, lower paper onto the patterned colors and then lift it off carefully. Rinse and hang up to dry.

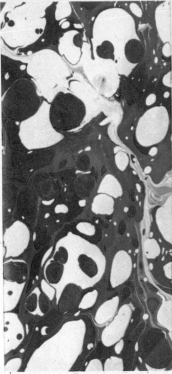
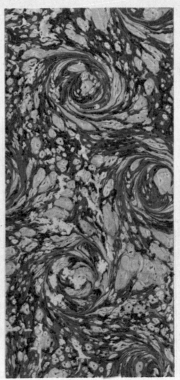
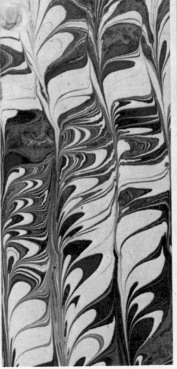
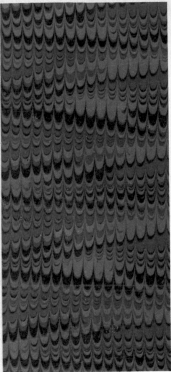

This pattern, called Turkish, is made by shaking colors on top of one another from a brush and then swirling until you like the result.

French curl is made by combing with ordinary marbling comb and then with wide-spaced comb in a circular motion.

Comb pattern is similar to that shown opposite and choice of color is a big factor in its success. Three is a good number to work.

Nonpareil. This is the finest of combed patterns and shows careful control. Use a closely-spaced comb for miniature waves.

around through the colors. You can thus arrange and rearrange them until you like the result.

☐ When ready, carefully lower the paper or other material, alum side downward, until it lies flat upon the surface of the size. Make sure you do not disturb the pattern or trap any air underneath the paper as this will prevent the sheet from touching the color and leave blank spaces.

The material only needs to remain a few seconds. Then gently lift it out, lay it on a draining board, pattern side up, and pour water across the surface to remove surplus size and color. Hang up to dry.

Special patterns

Over the many years that marbling has been practiced in different parts of the world a number of standard patterns have been handed down from one marbler to another. These patterns have attractive names like Turkish, Italian, Snail, Nonpareil, some of which clearly have some connection with their country of origin.

Many of these traditional patterns are formed by drawing a comb evenly across the surface of the size. Two such patterns, Nonpareil and Comb, are illustrated.

To make a comb, cut two pieces of cardboard to a length slightly shorter than the width of the tray and about 5cm (2″) wide.

Accurately measure 12mm ($\frac{1}{2}$″) or 2.5cm (1″) segments along the length of one piece of cardboard. Notch the surface at each line, deep enough to embed a pin or needle, and make each notch 2.5cm (1″) long as illustrated (fig.1).

Now embed 5cm (2″) needles in the slots, sticking them firmly with contact adhesive.

Glue the second cardboard strip against the first, with the needles in between, and place under a weight to dry. The needles will protrude 2.5cm (1″) beyond the cardboard.

You will find it useful to have two such combs, one with the teeth 2.5cm (1″) apart and one with 12mm ($\frac{1}{2}$″) gaps. Remember when marbling not to be disheartened by failure as there are many things that can and do go wrong. Marbling is an art and although quick success can often be gained, it takes practice to really master it. It will help if all the apparatus used for marbling is kept perfectly clean, the seaweed size prepared with considerable care and the colors thoroughly mixed and tested before beginning.

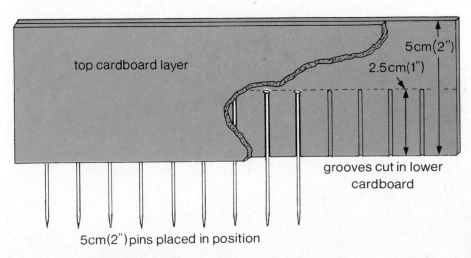

1. A marbling comb can be made at home using pins, cardboard and glue.

top cardboard layer

5cm(2″)
2.5cm(1″)

grooves cut in lower cardboard

5cm(2″)pins placed in position

Paul Williams

Dining chairs- spring and stuff

Cloth — upholstery 3

Victorian dining chairs can often be bought quite cheaply from a junk shop and you can turn them into something both useful and decorative simply by re-upholstering them and giving a little attention to the woodwork (see Renovation chapter 1, page 184). Their value can also increase by re-upholstering in the traditional way with springs and horsehair. Don't start by tackling antiques—anything over one hundred years old—that's a job for the experts. In this chapter a chair is stripped, the webbing replaced, the springs attached and the chair stuffed. In the next Upholstery chapter the edges are stitched, the second stuffing inserted and the chair finally covered with a top cover and finished off.

Tools

See Upholstery chapter 1, page 416. In addition you will need:

Coil springs: four 10cm (4″) in 12mm (10 gauge) wire.

Regulator. This is a type of needle 20cm -25cm (8″-10″) long which helps to form the stuffing into a good shape. It has one pointed and one flat end. A kitchen skewer could be used for this purpose, although if you are planning to do a lot of upholstery it is worth investing in the proper tool which is not expensive.

Needles. For making the bridles you will need a spring needle which is a heavy-duty needle 13cm (5″) long, curved along its length, so that it can be pulled in and out easily. For stitching the edge you will need a 25cm (10″) straight upholsterer's needle which is pointed at both ends.

Materials

Stuffing. Horsehair is the traditional stuffing but, because it is difficult and expensive to obtain today, it is often mixed with hog hair. Old hair mattresses can sometimes be bought cheaply at rummage sales or from junk shops. If you tease out the hair before washing it will return to its original life and springiness.

Alternatively, use Algerian fiber. This comes from the Algerian palm grass and, provided that it is teased out thoroughly, it makes a good, inexpensive stuffing.

For a small chair with about 7.5cm (3″) depth of padding you will need about 1kg (2lb) of either type of material.

Webbing. Buy sufficient to replace the original webbing; plain brown twill weave or upholsterer's webbing. Most ordinary chairs will need three or four strands of 5cm (2″) webbing placed back to front plus two strands across the seat.

Twine, a very strong, smooth string made from flax and hemp, is used for

These chairs (above and left) have been re-upholstered using traditional springing and stuffing techniques. This kind of chair is an ideal candidate for renovation and new upholstery and will give you many years of wear.

Nigel Messett

468

Stripping the upholstery: remove the tacks on the underside of the seat.

Underneath the top and inner covers there is a hair stuffing; lift this off.

Cut the stitching (above) and remove the twine holding the springs (below).

making bridle ties around the edge of the seat which help to hold the stuffing in place. Twine is also used for stitching on the springs and for stitching up the edge, another process which holds the stuffing in place and ensures a straight and firm edge.

Laid cord, a thicker twine, used for lashing the springs.

Scrim, a loosely woven material which is used for covering the first layer of stuffing. Allow enough to cut one piece the same size as the seat plus 15cm (6″) larger all around to allow for the depth of the padding.

Muslin is used for covering the second layer of stuffing; you will need a piece approximately the same size as the scrim.

Wadding is used over the muslin to prevent the stuffing from working through; allow the same amount as for the scrim.

Canvas, a heavy furnishing variety, is used over the springs. You will need a piece the size of the seat plus about 2.5cm (1″) all around for turnings.

Main cover. It's wise to choose a dark color in a proper upholstery grade fabric which will wear well and not show the dirt quickly. Patterned fabrics or those with a raised surface stay crisper-looking for longer than plain fabrics. Allow the same amount as for the scrim.

Stripping the upholstery

Follow the method described in Upholstery chapter 1, page 416. As you work make a note of the way the original top cover was attached, the number of springs and webbing strands and the height of the original padding. If you wish, the padding can be made a little higher or lower.

Check that all the old tacks have been removed from the frame. You should fill the old holes with plastic wood to give a firm basis for the tacks. Repair the frame and treat it for woodworm, if needed, and let the fluid dry completely before you start work.

The chair stripped of stuffing, springs and webbing. Take out remaining tacks.

Replacing the webbing

The webbing is the basis for the rest of the upholstery and must be secured tautly and really firmly. As the chair has springs the webbing is attached to the underside of the frame. You will find it easier to turn the chair upside down on the work surface.

Use the webbing straight from the roll. Without cutting it, fold over the end for 2.5cm (1″) and place it centrally on the back rail so the cut edge is uppermost and the fold is 1cm (½″) from the outer edge of the rail as shown in fig.1. Tack down, using five 15mm (⅝″) improved tacks placed in a row about 1cm (½″) from the fold, with the line of tacks staggered in the form of a shallow 'W'.

1.

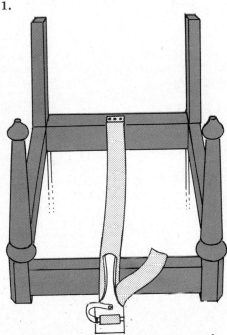

1. On a chair with a sprung seat webbing is attached to the underside of the frame. Tack down on the back rail and stretch the webbing across to the front using the web strainer.

If the wood tends to split use 1cm (½″) fine tacks instead (fig.1).

Stand on the opposite side of the chair by the front rail and, using the web strainer, put the webbing down in position on the front rail. Press the edge of the strainer on the side of the frame to give leverage. If the frame is polished use a pad of wadding to prevent damage from the strainer.

Tack down on the rail through the single thickness of webbing, using three tacks placed in a row.

Cut off the webbing 2.5cm (1″) from the tacks.

Turn back the excess over the tacks, placing them in a staggered 'W' formation as before.

Attach the remaining strands from the back to the front in the same way, then secure the side webbing (which runs

469

2a

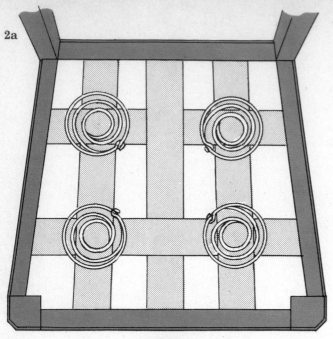

2b

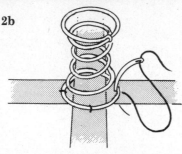

2. *The springs are arranged in a square on top of the webbing before sewing down with a spring needle and twine.*

3

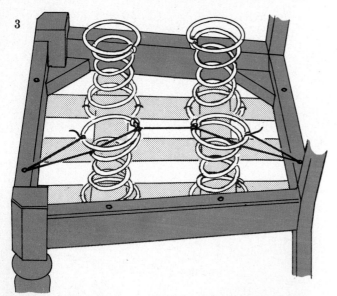

3. *Above: the springs are firmly lashed together with twine and attached to the frame to prevent them moving in the seat. Below: one way of winding twine around springs.*

4

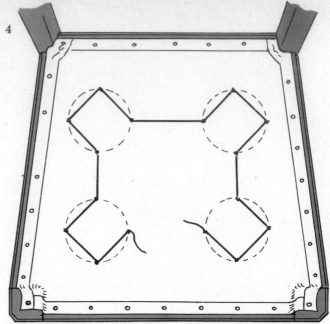

4. *The springs are covered with canvas and stitched in a similar way as they were attached to the webbing. Use the spring needle and make a single knot at each stitch.*

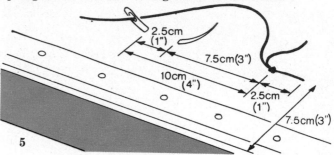

2.5cm (1")

7.5cm(3")

10cm (4")

2.5cm (1")

7.5cm(3")

5

5. *Bridle ties are stitched on the canvas to hold the stuffing.*

6

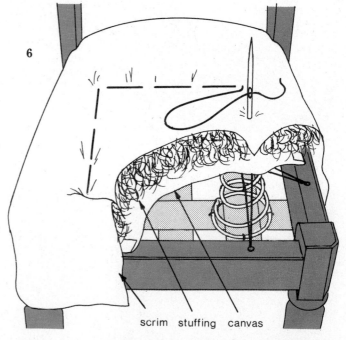

scrim stuffing canvas

6. *Stitch the scrim to the canvas with needle and twine. This process anchors the stuffing in middle of chair.*

across the seat), interlacing it with the first strands.

Attaching the springs

The springs must be sewn to the webbing, and then lashed together securely at the top to prevent them from moving about in the seat. This lashing also gives the chair a rounded shape.

Turn the chair the right way up and evenly space the springs in a square on top of the webbing intersections (fig. 2a).

The beginning and ends of the springs should be toward the middle.

Thread the spring needle with a long length of twine.

Using the fingers of your left hand to feel the positions of the spring from the underside of the chair, insert the needle into the webbing from underneath so that it comes out level with the outside of one spring. Pull the needle through, leaving a short tail of twine, and insert it into the webbing again from the top, catching the bottom ring of the spring with a single stitch (fig.2b).

Knot the tail of the twine to the length pulled through, but do not cut it.

Still with the needle on the underside of the chair, move to the other side of the ring and stitch it to the webbing there.

Move back to the outside again and make another stitch. This makes three stitches in all, in a 'V'-shape.

Without cutting the twine move to the next spring and repeat the operation. **Continue around in this way for the** remaining springs then make a knot to finish off and cut the twine.

Lashing the springs. Attach two 15mm ($\frac{5}{8}$") improved tacks on all four sides of the frame, each one in line with the center of a spring, hammering them half-way in.

Cut off enough cord to stretch twice around the frame. Leaving a tail which will stretch easily to the top of the nearest spring, plus a couple of inches for knotting, tie the cord around a tack on the back rail, and hammer the tack in.

Working toward the front of the chair, take the main length of cord to the nearest spring and knot it around the coil which is second from the top of the nearest side. Take it through the spring to the other side and knot it around the top coil. Use a clovehitch knot (fig.7).

Move to the other spring in the row and knot the cord around the top coil on the nearest side, keeping the distance between the springs the same as at the bottom. Take the cord through the spring and knot it around the coil which is second from the top on the front edge. Tie it off tightly around tack on front rail and hammer in (fig.3).

Take the tail of cord at each tack back to the nearest spring and tie it around the top coil on the outside, pulling tightly so that the spring slightly leans down toward the frame.

Repeat this process on the other pair of springs with the cord running parallel to the first length, and then again with two lengths running across the chair. The springs will now have a rounded shape.

The main stuffing

The canvas. Center this over the springs. Fold over 2.5cm (1") on one side of the canvas and place this centrally on the back rail with the raw edge uppermost. Tack down 15mm ($\frac{5}{8}$") tacks, placing them 2.5cm (1") apart and 1cm ($\frac{1}{2}$") from the fold. Fit it neatly around the back uprights, cutting if necessary, as described in Upholstery chapter 2, page 434.

Smooth the canvas over the springs by pulling it quite taut and temporarily tack it to the front rail through a single thickness, keeping the grain of canvas

7.

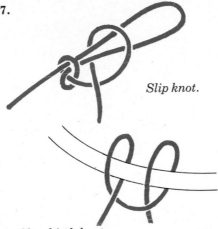

Slip knot.

Clovehitch knot.

absolutely straight. Smooth out the canvas to the side rails, and temporarily tack through the single thickness.

When satisfied that the canvas is completely smooth and the grain straight, hammer the tacks in completely. Trim off the excess canvas to within 2.5cm (1") of the tacks, then fold this over and tack it down at about 5cm (2") intervals.

Stitch the springs to the canvas in a similar way as they were attached to the webbing, but make a single knot at each stitch to lock it in position (fig.4).

To make bridle ties for the stuffing, thread the spring needle with enough twine to go 1½ times round the chair. The stitch used is rather similar to back stitch. Start by making a stitch in the canvas about 2.5cm (1") long and 2.5cm (1") from the edge. Pull it through, leaving a 7.5cm (3") tail. Tie the tail in a slip knot (fig.7) to the main length at

the point where it emerges from the canvas.

Go forward and insert the needle about 10cm (4") away, but pointing it backward. Pull it out about 7.5cm (3") from the starting point (fig.5). Leave the stitch on top of the canvas loose enough for a hand to be inserted.

Continue around the whole edge in this way, making sure that a 2.5cm (1") stitch falls at each corner. You may have to adjust the length of the bridles to do this.

Finish off by tying a knot.

Stuffing. Take a handful of stuffing and tease it out thoroughly, removing any lumpy pieces. Put it under one of the bridle threads, working it together well to prevent lumps. Do this for all the bridles, then fill the middle with more stuffing, teasing it well to make an even shape and to overhang the edge slightly by the same amount all around.

Scrim. Place it centrally over the stuffing and fix one temporary tack in the middle of each side to hold it Put two other temporary tacks on each side of the central tack. At this stage the scrim should be rather loose on the surface of the stuffing.

Thread an upholsterer's needle with a long piece of twine and stitch through from the scrim to the canvas in a rectangle about 7.5cm (3") from the edges of the seat. To do this, pass the needle through the scrim and stuffing and pull it out between the webbing on the underside of the chair, leaving a tail of twine on top for tying off. As soon as the needle is completely through the canvas, keep the unthreaded end pointing down, and push needle back through the canvas with the threaded end 1cm ($\frac{1}{2}$") further on. Withdraw it on top and tie to the main length in a slip knot.

Push the needle back into the scrim making a stitch about 7.5cm (3") long on top. Continue around in this way, leaving a 1cm ($\frac{1}{2}$") gap between stitches (fig.6).

Pull the twine tightly so that the scrim is pulled down and be careful not to catch the springs as the needle passes through. Even out any lumps in the stuffing with the regulator. This process anchors the hair in the middle.

Remove the temporary tacks securing the scrim to the frame—on the front of the seat first, then the sides, and lastly the back. Even out the hair which is along the edges of the seat. Add more if necessary to make a fat roll which just protrudes beyond the edge of the frame. Tuck the raw edge of the scrim under the hair, smoothing it over the roll. Use 10mm ($\frac{3}{8}$") tacks to fix the folded edge of the scrim to the chamfered edge of the frame. Do not pull it too tightly over the roll.

Arranging flowers at home

Flowers and plants 1

Anyone who is fascinated by color and finds enjoyment in mixing different hues and blending new shades with existing ones—anyone in fact, who loves decoration and design—will find infinite pleasure in arranging flowers. It is one of the most decorative of the decorative arts.

You cannot keep rearranging a room all the time but you can make significant changes in it simply by rearranging the flowers. How you arrange them, the colors you choose, their size, the containers you put them in, all result in subtle or dramatic variations in mood and appearance. But just as your surroundings reflect your needs and individual style, so flowers should reflect the room's and this is the most important thing to bear in mind when arranging any flowers—that they must eventually become part of a room. They cannot exist simply as 'an arrangement'.

These chapters compare and explain several styles of flower arranging—the traditional, more formal style developed into an art by Constance Spry; Ikebana, the Japanese art of using a very few elements to poetic

Stems become part of the arrangement when a glass vase is used.

Steve Bicknell

effect, and the modern, informal and apparently very simple way of handling flowers which is the subject of this chapter and is typified in the work of designer David Hicks.

Flowers and background

Styles of flower arrangement change with styles of home decoration and today the keynote is informality. Rigid, symmetrical lines have been replaced by more gentle contours and damask has given way to printed cottons.

Where simplicity and ease prevail these should be reflected in the flowers in a room. But there's more to apparent simplicity than meets the eye—the main thing being a good sense of proportion.

You are limited by four main considerations: the flowers available, the colors and spaces in your home, the containers you have and the reservoir of your own ideas. It also helps to learn to care for flowers properly, as arrangements can last twice as long with proper attention from the start.

Selecting flowers

The flowers you use depends largely on where you live, whether in town or in the country, and what time of year it is. But before you buy or pick flowers, even when they are in abundance, it makes sense to think about where you are going to put them, since both the color and the size of the arrangement will be affected. A large, massed arrangement, for instance, requires an area such as a chest or table without a lamp on it, and colors must work together and also contribute to the room. In winter, when flowers are scarce and expensive, it is a good rule to stick to small arrangements of a few flowers of one kind such as carnations. Even one flower in the right container can make a successful arrangement, adding just the degree of color needed for a finishing touch.

Expensive winter flowers can also be filled out with greenery, but really large spaces are probably best filled at this time of year with dried arrangements.

Preparing flowers

Florist's flowers. Buy flowers still in

bud if you can and avoid any with centers that look over-mature (blowzy) with loose pollen, too dark in color) or have drooping edges and leaves. As soon as you get them home, trim a thumbnail's length off the stems by making a slanting cut and plunge the stems into tepid water to soak.

Garden flowers. Pick garden flowers before they are fully open and never during the full heat of a summer day. Never twist or pull the stem off but cut with special flower scissors, making a slanting, rather than straight, cut. Lupins are an exception in that they should be cut straight across.

If you are picking many flowers then put a bucket of water in a shady place and put them into it as you cut. Plants, quite naturally, are shocked by cutting and jostling but gentle treatment seems to mollify them.

Wild flowers. These are the most delicate of all to maintain but the effort is well worth it. Go collecting equipped with a roll of kitchen foil, paper towels and a bottle of water. Wrap the stems in dampened paper and then cover with kitchen foil. Keep flowers out of the sun as much as possible after picking. Alternatively, tie them up in large **plastic bags.**

Prolonging life

A little extra care is well worth it in the response which flowers make, keeping their heads erect and leaves crisp and often doubling their longevity.

Water. Soaking flowers up to their necks for several hours or overnight is a good thing to do before starting to arrange them in a container. Leaves (except for velvety ones) can also be submerged. Soft rain-water from a rain butt is ideal. All water should be at room temperature before you put flowers in it.

Always arrange flowers in tepid water —a small piece of charcoal in the container will keep the water pure.

Most flowers, except those that exude a sticky substance, such as daffodils, will last longer if you add some sugar to the water—two teaspoons to 0.5lit (1pt). *Daffodils* and *narcissi* can last very well in little water, as long as they do not go dry, but *hellebore* need deep water, or to be floated in a bowl. *Holly* is best without any water at all. But apart from a few exceptions plants are not particularly fussy about exactly how much water they are arranged in. The water in vases should be topped up every day with fresh water at room temperature.

Stems. *Lilac*, *roses* and *chrysanthemums* should all be hammered and split about 2.5cm (1″) up the stem to let the water in.

Stems which exude a white juice, such as *poppies* and *dahlias*, should be put

in a few inches of boiling water for about ten seconds to disperse the juice. Protect the heads by covering them with a cloth. Poppies can be discouraged from fading by charring the ends of the stalks.

Tulips only drink through the green part of their stems so cut off any white part at the base. They also tend to droop when arranged, and wrapping stems in newspaper up to the heads (putting no more than six in each bunch) before soaking them helps stiffen them. It's said also that tulips straighten up when they see themselves in a mirror.

Wallflowers will die quickly on long stems, so cut them quite short.

Daffodils and *narcissi* exude a sticky substance. Hold the stems under running water to remove it. This juice

The stylosa iris, arranged by David Hicks, illustrates basic principles of arranging flowers in the modern home. It is simple, natural looking and blends superbly with its surroundings.

is harmful to other flowers so try to segregate this group or, alternatively, soak them for at least six hours before combining them with other flowers.

If you cut *broom* when it is in flower put the stems in very hot water before arranging it.

Carnation stems should be broken between the joints, not at the joints.

Delphiniums and *lupins* last longer if their hollow stems are up-ended and filled with water after they are cut. Plug the stems with cotton and leave overnight in deep water.

Cut *hydrangeas* on the new wood.

Before arranging them, place the stems in boiling water for a few seconds. Then soak the flower heads in tepid water.

Hydrangeas absorb water through the flower heads, so it helps to spray them frequently after they have been arranged. *Mimosa* also lasts longer if sprayed in this way. *Iris* stems contain a lot of water and it is evaporation that causes them to droop. When picked, wrap each head in soft paper and place the flowers in deep water. Leave in a cool place for a few hours.

Polyanthus lasts better if the stems are cut short and the flowers grouped together in a bunch.

Leaves. Although it is correct to soak flowers with leaves submerged, always remove any leaves below the water line before you put them in a container.

473

Leaves take up, unnecessarily, space and water. They also tend to discolor the water and make it smell foul. Thin out excess foliage so that flower heads are not starved of water.

Basic equipment

Flower scissors (fig.1a) are an invaluable tool as their serrated edges make it possible to cut flowers, tough wood stems and wire mesh used in containers. **Wire mesh** (fig.1b) is obtained at most gardening and some hardware shops and should be plastic coated, if possible, since this does not rust. Wire with 5cm (2″) holes is the most useful, and crumpled balls of it are excellent for holding arrangements erect. A little practice is needed, however, to get the right amount of mesh for the size of the vase and the flowers which need support. More than one layer of wire is necessary in tall vases and you will need to align the holes so that the flowers will go all the way into the container.

Pin holders (fig.1c) are small round

1b. *wire mesh.*

1c. *pin holder.*

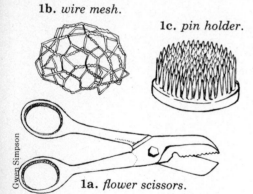

Gwen Simpson

1a. *flower scissors.*

beds of nails that can be bought in several sizes and provide useful anchors for many kinds of arrangements. Put them into the container before the water and stick each stem securely into the nails. Sometimes it is necessary to attach the pin holder to the container with a bit of plasticine to keep it from sliding about.

Even the smartest pin holder is less attractive than flower stems so avoid using them in clear glass vases.

Containers

Choosing the right container is one of the most important elements in flower arranging for if it is wrong, then so will everything else be.

Containers should by no means be limited to those designed specially to hold flowers. They can be improvised from any number of household objects —imagine an earthenware jug full of wild flowers or a teapot full of sweet peas. Wicker baskets make very effective containers provided you use old cans as liners.

Glass containers are another intrigu-

right

The arrangements shown here all use the same two containers, yet considerable flexibility of style is possible with different flowers and stem lengths.

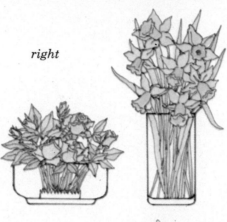

right

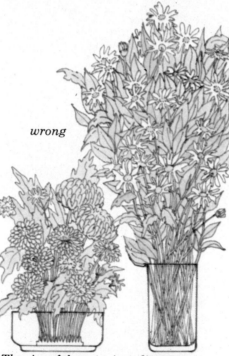

wrong

The size of the container dictates to some extent the size and shape of the arrangement. Both arrangements above are too large and overpowering for their containers.

ing possibility since the stems of flowers become part of the total line of the arrangement. A number of clear or tinted glass containers can be quickly obtained with a bottle cutting device. By sawing off the top at the

desired place you get containers of different heights and shapes.

Bowls of all sorts can be used to hold flowers when a pin holder or mesh is used for support, but shallow arrangements as a rule do not last as long as others.

Proportion. Texture and color are of immense importance in a container and so is size. As a general rule, in tall arrangements (but not large round ones) flowers should not protrude more than 50% above the top of the container. Tall flowers look ridiculous in a short, stocky vase but the reverse is not true. It is perfectly permissible to have only the heads of flowers protruding beyond the lip of a tall vase. You will find you have many more creative possibilities working with flowers if you keep a selection of containers in the sizes, colors and textures which lend themselves to the mood of your home. Store them on a shelf or in a cupboard where you can tell at a glance what might and might not do. A list of improvised containers — eg silver coffee pot, galvanized pail, china cream pitcher—tucked inside the cupboard door will serve as a useful reminder of possibilities. A large part of thinking up ideas is, after all, having a quick cross-reference of the alternatives.

Color

There is perhaps nothing in nature that is as ornamental as flowers and when you think of arranging them, try thinking about them in their natural state first, not in an orderly planted garden but in a field. Cast your mind back to fields of flowers or herbaceous borders you have seen and this will give you some idea of the tremendous scope you have in mixing and combining different colors and flowers in your home.

When buying flowers it is a good idea to keep these thoughts in mind and never buy the same number of each kind of flower, rather choose a dozen of one kind and perhaps half a dozen of another. If they can be bought singly get odd numbers. These will give you a more 'natural' look.

Making arrangements

By no means confine your efforts to putting flowers in a container one at a time although this may be necessary in those requiring a pin holder or wire mesh. Trim the lengths fairly evenly and try sticking a bunch into a vase all at once—giving a gentle shake—to get a natural look. If you are using greenery, stick it in amongst the flowers instead of 'backing them up' with it.

Remember that flowers are fragile and need gentle handling. Camellias and gardenias for example bruise easily and should be touched as little as possible. Most flowers do best if any dead heads are removed—even freesias last longer this way—and it encourages other buds to open.

Laying down too many rules about arranging flowers defeats the whole concept of informality and whether or not you are successful with flowers depends as much on spontaneity as on anything. So don't be afraid to experiment, but bear in mind at the same time the basic guidelines about using display space and determining the mood of a room. A bunch of daisies in the hands of six different people can clearly express six different personalities, provided each person has a definite idea of what they want the flowers to 'say'. This is far more important than any involved techniques. It is always worth reading books on flower arrangement, visiting flower shows and joining flower clubs, but in the end your own personal taste ought to be your best guide.

right

wrong

Where an arrangement will be put is of prime importance in its planning. The two arrangements above are in proportion to the size of their containers. But the one on the right is the wrong size for the table it is on. It vies with the lamp and at the same time obscures the picture on the wall.

Summer colors are the outstanding feature of the arrangement by David Hicks shown below. It is shaped like a nosegay, spilling over with blossoms of all different sizes. The careful lack of symmetry and slight unevenness of shape all contribute to its lightness of mood.

475

Accent colors

This pink and yellow flower is already bright. A dull color could accent it.

You may have produced a perfectly pleasant scheme based on variations of one color (see Design know-how chapter 13, page 364) or related colors (see Design know-how chapter 14, page 392). But somehow, something is missing. It's nice, but dull. What you probably need is an accent color.

What is an accent color? An accent color is usually bright and intense and is used in small amounts to give a flash of brilliance, of excitement. It may be a complementary color, ie a streak of yellow in a violet scheme. Or you may find that a clashing color (ie a discordant color) works.

Using one accent. You might be making a necklace with lovely natural-colored wooden or shell beads, and just add one or two turquoise beads to liven the whole thing up. The same kind of turquoise blue would be an accent if introduced into knitting or weaving made up of predominantly soft blues and mauves.

Using more than one accent. In something larger or more complex, for example a room scheme or a patchwork, you may need to introduce an accent in more than one place. A patchwork made up predominantly of blues and greens may need accent colors at irregular intervals—say, yellow or sharp pink—to enliven it. It's a question of balance, which is discussed more fully in a later chapter.

Using black and white. When a color doesn't seem to be the answer you may find that a judicious use of black and white will work. Both are very effective, so beware of using too much.

Key points. There will probably be features in your craft work which you wish to highlight and bring into prominence, for example the buttons of a dress, the wheels of a toy, the central motif in a necklace. Use an accent color and be sure that everybody will notice this feature.

Start by experimenting with the color schemes illustrated here. First of all cut out a 'window' in a sheet of black or white paper so you can isolate each example. Now find some patches in a color magazine similar to the accent colors shown and cut them out

roughly to fit the areas marked with a question mark. Now try out various accents with each scheme until you're satisfied. If you don't like the suggestions given, try your own.

An accent color can give sparkle to low-intensity blues and grays.

Victoria Drew

In a complicated design you could choose more than one accent color.

In a monochromatic scheme you have a wide choice of bright accents.

A discordant or contrast color may work in a predominantly red or blue scheme.

These accent colors are bright and lively; or choose black and white instead.

476

Creative ideas 17

Glittering line designs

There are two ways to apply glitter in line designs. You can draw the design in clear adhesive then sprinkle on loose glitter. Allow the adhesive to dry and then carefully shake off and collect the excess glitter for re-use.

The alternative, and simpler method, is to use a commercially available glitter which is a mixture of clear adhesive and glitter, contained in a tube which has a special nozzle so that you can literally squeeze the design onto the object to be decorated.

Besides the obvious appeal of commercial glitter, it has the advantage that it will adhere to practically any surface except polystyrene and plastic.

These heart-shaped pouches for hankies, stockings or panty hose are made from felt. First cut out the shapes, then stitch them together and press.

Draw the design you have chosen in tailor's chalk on the felt and simply squeeze the glitter onto the lines. Leave to dry thoroughly.

Designed by Anthony Wilson.

Steve Bicknell

Taped boxes with separate lids

Square boxes with lids

☐ Draw pattern in fig.1 on cardboard.
☐ Cut out the box with a sharp cutting tool, cutting along solid lines and scoring along the dotted lines.

Chapter 12, page 422, gives details of the sort of cardboard to use for box making, the techniques of scoring, cutting and sticking boxes and the importance of ensuring that all angles are 90° (Design know-how Chapter 1, page 28). You will need all this information to make the following boxes.

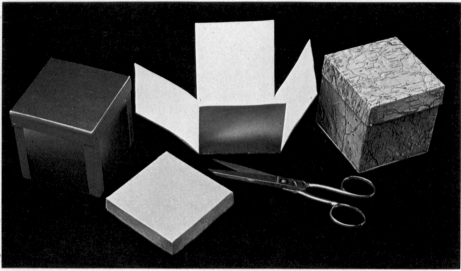

Covered square boxes with separate lids are very easy to make and assemble.

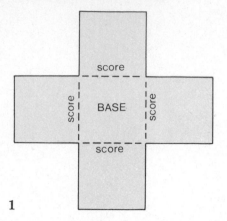

1

☐ Fold up the side pieces on scored lines to form the box.
☐ Hold the corners together on the outside of the box with decorative adhesive tape (fig.2).

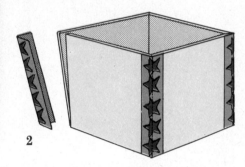

2

To make a lid draw the pattern in fig.3 but make the center square 1.6mm ($\frac{1}{16}''$) larger all around than the base of the box, so that the lid fits comfortably over the box.
Make the side pieces as deep as you like, from 6mm ($\frac{1}{4}''$) to 2.5cm (1'') or more.
☐ Finish the lid by sticking adhesive tape all around the outside (fig.4) or on the corners only.

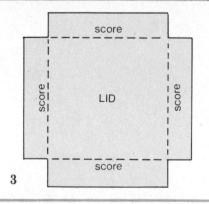

3

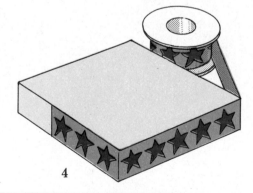

4

☐ It's a simple matter to adapt the pattern to make an oblong box, or one that is shallow or deep (fig.5).
The sides must all be the same depth and the lid must be at least 1.6mm ($\frac{1}{16}''$) bigger overall than the base.

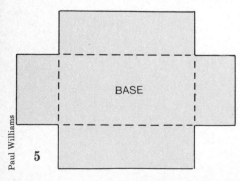

5

Roger Phillips

Paul Williams

Decorative paper cover

Lay the cut-out shape of the box, scored side down, on the wrong side of the decorative paper. Stick and press down smoothly. Don't leave the covering paper to dry out completely or the paper may tear. When the paper is almost dry, cut all around the shape (fig.6), either right to the edge of the box or else leave a margin of 1.3cm (½") at the top of the sides to be turned over. (If you do this, allow for the extra thickness when making the lid).

□ Gently fold up the scored sides to avoid tearing the paper.

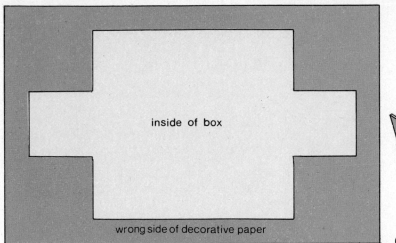

inside of box

wrong side of decorative paper

6

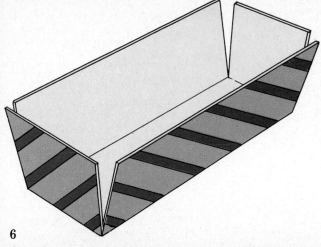

Lining square boxes

Both bought and hand-made boxes look especially glamorous if they are lined with beautiful papers. Try a matt gold paper inside a box covered in a tortoise-shell paper, a marbled paper inside a deeper colored box, or a plain plush paper inside a box covered in a rich, gold-embossed paper.

□ Cut a piece of paper the same dimensions as the box, with small tabs on any two sides. Fold in the same way as for box and stick the lining to the inside of the box by the tabs. Stick the lining to the inside of the top of the box as well.

□ To line with cardboard, cut the vertical measurement of the lining slightly smaller than the box to allow for the thickness of the cardboard.

A group of three boxes, sumptuously trimmed and decorated.

Roger Phillips

Compartments for boxes

The easiest way to make compartments for square boxes is to cut them out of interlocking sections of cardboard. The strips of cardboard should be as high, long and wide as inside of box.

□ Cut slots half-way up the strips and slot them into each other (fig.7).

□ For long boxes, make compartments of folded cardboard, scoring the top sides and the underside of the cardboard as shown (fig.8) to form peaks the same height as the box. Make as many compartments as you need from one long strip the width of the box, then drop it into the box.

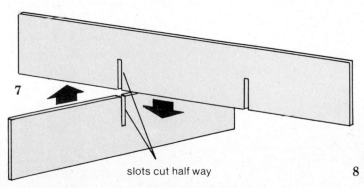

7

slots cut half way

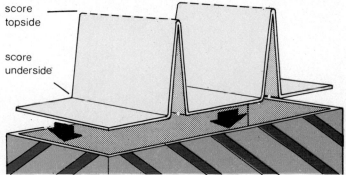

score topside

score underside

8

Colored resin panels

Panels made from resin in such a way as to look like stained glass can be very attractive. Designs using translucent colors are particularly effective and can be made to cover a small bathroom window instead of the usual curtaining, or as a cupboard door with a light behind it. Such a panel can be made to the exact size required. The same method can also be used to decorate mirrors, or small pieces can be adapted for jewelry.

It is fairly easy to mold the panels or curve them, so they can even be shaped to form a lampshade.

The strength of a panel depends on its size and thickness. Small pieces used for jewelry will not need any support, nor will slightly larger ones for mobiles. Larger panels should be attached to glass or reinforced with a framework, depending on their use.

Shrinkage can be a problem if you want to fit a panel exactly to a particular size. To overcome this you can make the panel slightly larger, say 6mm ($\frac{1}{4}''$) all around, and then sand off any excess, if necessary. Alternatively, make the panel to the size you want and, when it is completely cured, add a surrounding resin border to compensate for the shrinkage. The shrinkage will vary between different brands of resin and it also depends on the amount of catalyst used.

The technique used to create the panels involves a number of stages, First, a design must be traced onto a layer of wax. The lines are cut out with a linoleum-cutting tool and the lines are then filled with resin. You can color the resin black to simulate leading, or use it clear. When this framework has cured it is removed from the wax and the sections within the framework are filled with colored resin.

The cured panel is then mounted onto glass or whatever finished surface is desired.

The materials involved to make the panel are resin, catalyst and color pigments. The wax base is not part of the completed panel and can be melted down and re-used over and over.

Do not use the type of resin used for cold enameling as it takes a very long time to dry.

To make a panel

You will need:

Casting resin; catalyst or hardener.
Color pigments.
Beeswax—candle wax will do.
Polyester film—you can use aluminum foil but it punctures very easily and if a leak does occur the whole piece will be ruined as you cannot remove the aluminum foil.
Paper cups and stirrers.
Medium and fine grade wet and dry paper.
Shallow baking tray.
Linoleum-cutting tools—the front end of a pointed potato peeler can be used.
Screwdriver.
Tracing paper.

☐ Melt the wax and pour it into the baking tray. The wax should not be less than 6mm ($\frac{1}{4}''$) deep.

☐ Transfer design to tracing paper. Place paper on the wax and lightly trace over design to leave an imprint.

☐ Use the linoleum-cutting tool or potato peeler to cut out grooves in the wax about 6mm ($\frac{1}{4}''$) deep (fig.1).

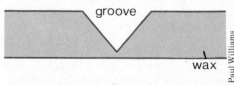

1. *Above: the groove cut into the wax.*

Left: the resin panels make attractive decorations. Designer Margaret Rogers.

Paul Williams

Tracing the design onto the wax.

Cutting out the grooves in the wax.

Filling the grooves with resin.

Cover the design with polyester film.

The sections are filled with resin.

Panel soaked in hot water being shaped.

The grooves can be smoothed by heating a screwdriver and running it over the surface of the grooves.

☐ Mix the resin and catalyst or hardener. Add color pigment first if you want to color the outlines, eg black to simulate leading.

☐ Pour the resin into the grooves, making sure that the resin is evenly spread and that all the grooves have been filled. If you make black outlines make sure that they are neat and do not overflow onto the sections.

☐ When the grooves have cured, apply a thin coat of resin to the surface of the grooves and cover the design with the polyester film or aluminum foil.

☐ To remove the cast grooves from the wax, heat the wax gently, and carefully peel off the polyester film with the resin adhering to it. The resin framework is reasonably flexible at this stage and should be handled gently. Place the polyester film on a flat working surface with the resin facing upward.

☐ Mix resin, catalyst and color pigments and fill the sections between the resin framework in colors of your choice. Fill each section to the top, but do not let it overflow into another section as it will spoil the color effect.

☐ When the resin has cured, the polyester film is pulled away.

☐ The outer edge can be smoothed with medium grade wet and dry paper. Remove any sharp bits and then smooth and level the top surface by wrapping medium wet and dry paper around a small block of wood and rubbing it down.

☐ Finish with a fine grade wet and dry paper and wash off any dust.

☐ Mix a small quantity of clear resin with a slightly higher proportion of catalyst than before and apply this thinly to the top surface. This will restore a shiny finish to the transparent surface.

☐ Leave in a warm place to cure.

☐ To mount the panel onto glass or any other surface, mix some resin and catalyst and use this as glue.

To make a hole in the panel, if required, push a hot needle or knitting needle through it.

To bend or curve a panel. Hold it in front of a heater or radiator and, as it warms, form the slope required and then run it under cold water. To do this successfully the panel should be fairly thin.

Panels can also be immersed in very hot water, taken out, shaped and then held in cold water to retain their shape. The panels might show slight imperfections after being curved. If you sand the surfaces smooth before curving and cover with transparent resin after curving, as mentioned above, the surface will be restored.

General Hints

Always let the resin cure in a dust-free atmosphere.

Do not handle it while it is still sticky as it will spoil the surface. The exposed surface takes some time to dry so be patient.

The more color pigment you add the longer the resin takes to cure.

The shaped panels can be combined into a lampshade. Left: tracing pattern.

Paul Williams

Dick Miller

Trevor Lawrence

481

Edgings and insertions

This chapter explains how to make fringes, and then goes on to show how bands and motifs can be combined to make all sorts of edgings and insertions which can do so much to enrich a shawl, a dress or a scarf.

Fringing

Fringes are particularly effective if they are made luxuriously long or thick. You can use them to lengthen last year's skirt, to change the proportions of a bag, or to give a final flourish to a fashionable scarf, whether it's silky and summery, or made of heavy, winter-weight wool.

Cut multiples of 3 or more strands of yarn into lengths twice the length of the fringe for each group of fringe. Divide the strands into groups of 3 or more and fold them in half. Using a crochet hook and with WS of work facing, draw the folded loops through the edge of the fabric (fig.1). Place all the ends over the hook and draw them through the loops on the hook, then pull up tightly (fig.2). Repeat evenly along the edge of the fabric.

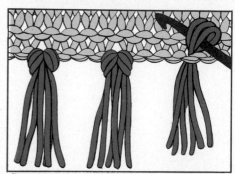

Drawing folded strands through fabric.

Pulling strands through loop on hook.

Lattice fringing

Cut the strands into lengths 2½ times the finished length of the lattice fringe. Mount the strands and work as given for fringing along the edge of the fabric. Take half the number of strands of one group of fringe and half the number of strands of the next group and make an overhand knot with these about 2.5cm (1″) away from the previous knot. Take the remaining strands of the group and half the strands of the next group and knot them together in the same way. Continue knotting half the strands of one group to half the strands of the next group. Return to the beginning of the fringing, take half the strands of one group and knot them together with half the strands of the next group, about 2.5cm (1″) down from the previous knot. Continue in this way to complete the lattice effect. This process can be repeated as often as desired.

Interesting fringes, simply created with knots and crochet hook.

Melvin Grey

To make a treble

Make desired number of chains plus 4 extra chains to count as turning chain, which is required at beginning of every row of the treble to bring hook up to correct height to work the first stitch.

1st row. *Yarn around hook twice, insert hook from front to back into fifth chain stitch from hook (fig.1), yarn around hook (fig.2) and draw loop through chain stitch (fig.3), yarn around hook and draw through 2 loops on hook (figs. 4, 5 and 6) 3 times*. One treble has been made, plus first skipped 4 chain stitches which count as first treble, leaving one loop on hook. Repeat from * to * but working into next and every chain stitch to end.

On next and every following row turn the work so that the yarn is again in position at the beginning of the row, make 4 chain to count as the first treble, skip the first treble of previous row, work 1 treble into each treble to end, inserting the hook under the top 2 loops of treble in the previous row.

These six stages show how to begin working your first row in treble. The four chain skipped at the start of the row become your first stitch.

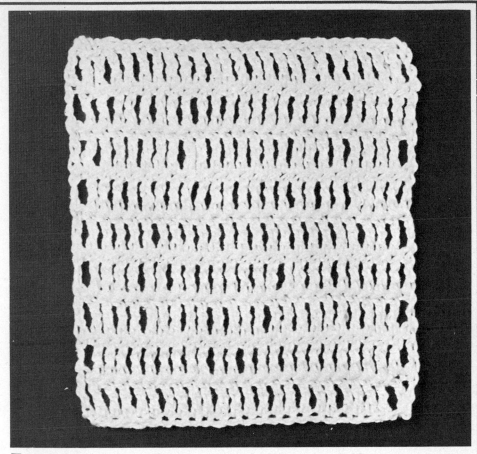

Trebles make a neat and slightly open fabric that grows quickly.

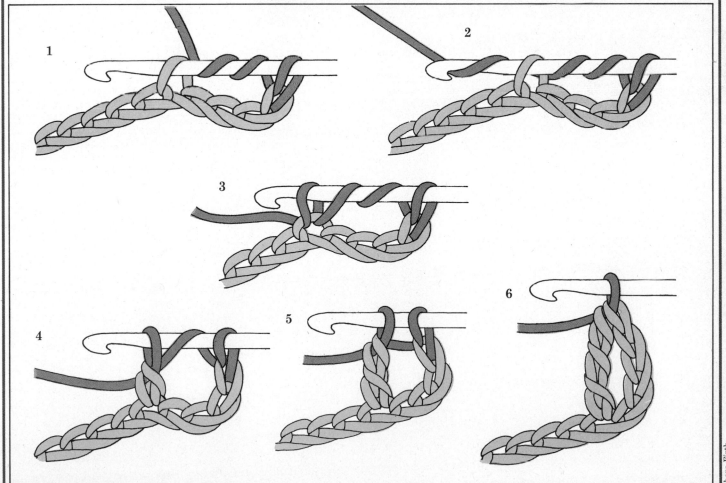

483

Daisy edging used to trim a lampshade, showing the leaves and stems which join the flowers together.

Edgings and insertions

The daisy chains given here can be bordered on one or both sides with rows of trebles, and once you have got the technique of combining motifs to make a border you can add the motifs in the last chapters with bands to build up borders of your own.

Insertions can be used to make a plain dress prettier by adding them into the bodice, sleeves or along the seam lines. Or use insertions to let out dresses that are too small or to lengthen sleeves and skirts that are too short—ideal for growing girls.

Daisy chains

This idea can be adapted for many different uses. The complete edging can be extended to fit around a table cloth or to trim an evening shawl. Worked in heavier cotton yarn, the border only could be made into a crisp, summer belt. Each motif can be used separately as hair ornaments, lapel brooches, to trim napkin rings or, alternatively, sewn onto blouses and sweaters.

Daisy lampshade edging

To fit a shade approximately 91cm (36")
around the lower edge.
You will need:
50gm (1¾oz) No.20 cotton yarn.
One No.1.00 ISR (US size B) crochet hook.
Note: One patt rep consists of one
complete daisy point of one large daisy, 2 medium daisies, 1 small daisy, 1 stem and 2 leaves worked onto the edge of the straight daisy border, which consists of 5 small daisies measuring approximately 15cm (6") when joined tog.

Small daisy border

Using No.1.00 ISR (US size B) hook make 7ch. Join with a sl/st to first ch to form circle.
1st round. 3ch, work 17dc into circle. Join with a sl/st to third of first 3ch. 18dc.
2nd round. *3ch, skip next 2dc of previous round, 1sl/st into next dc, rep from * 4 times more, 3ch. Join with a sl/st to first of first 3ch. 6 loops.
3rd round. Into each 3ch loop work (1sc, 1hdc, 3dc, 1hdc, 1sc). Join with a sl/st to first sc. Fasten off.
Make 29 more small daises in same way. Join into one strip, joining side petals of one daisy to side petals of next.

Daisy border edging

With WS of daisy border facing, rejoin yarn with a sl/st to center top of first petal of first daisy, 5ch, 1sc into center of next petal of same daisy, 5ch, *1sc into center of first petal of
next daisy, 5ch, 1sc into center of next petal of same daisy, 5ch, rep from * to end, omitting last 5ch at end of last rep. Turn.
Next row. 3ch to count as first dc, *work 1dc into each of next 5ch picking up back loops only, 1dc into sc picking up back loop only, rep from * to end. Fasten off.
Turn and work along other edge of daisy petals in same way.

Daisy points

Work 6 small daisies as given for border.

Medium daisy

Using No.1.00 ISR (US size B) hook make 11ch. Join with a sl/st to first ch to form circle.
1st round. 3ch to count as first dc, work 31dc into circle. Join with a sl/st to 3rd of first 3ch. 32dc.
2nd round. *4ch, skip 3dc of previous round, 1sl/st into next dc, rep from * 6 times more, 4ch, skip 3dc. Join with a sl/st to first of 4ch. 8 loops.
3rd round. Into each 4ch loop work (1sc, 1hdc, 3dc, 1hdc, 1sc). Join with a sl/st to first sc. 8 petals.
4th round. *4ch, 1sl/st into back loop of st on second round between next 2 petals, rep from * 7 times more, joining last sl/st into first of first 4ch.
5th round. Into each 4ch loop work (1sc, 1hdc, 5dc, 1hdc, 1sc). Join with a sl/st to first sc. Fasten off.
Work 11 more medium daisies in same way.

Large daisy

Work first 5 rounds as given for medium daisy.
6th round. *5ch, 1sl/st into back of st on 4th round between next 2 petals, rep from * 7 times more, joining last sl/st into first of first 5ch.
7th round. Into each 5ch loop work (1sc, 1hdc, 2dc, 5tr, 2dc, 1hdc, 1sc). Join with a sl/st to first sc. Fasten off. Make 5 more large daisies in same way.

To complete

Sew 2 petals of each small daisy to edge below every fifth daisy on border. Sew one medium daisy to next petal on each side of small daisy. Sew one large daisy between each 2 medium daisies. Join border into circle and stitch in place around lower edge of lampshade.

Stem and leaves

Rejoin yarn to center of top petal of large daisy with a sl/st, work 9ch for stem, 1sl/st into dc edge immediately above center flower to right of stem, turn and work 13ch, sl/st to petal of next daisy, work back along 13ch as foll:- 1sc, 1hdc, 3dc, 3tr, 3dc, 1hdc, 1sc, 1sl/st into stem on edge, work 13ch for leaf at left side, 1sl/st into petal top of medium daisy at left side of stem, turn and work into 13ch as foll:- 1sc, 1hdc, 3dc, 3tr, 3dc, 1hdc, 1sc, 1sl/st into top of stem. Fasten off.
Complete 5 other sections in same way.

Alasdair Ogilvie

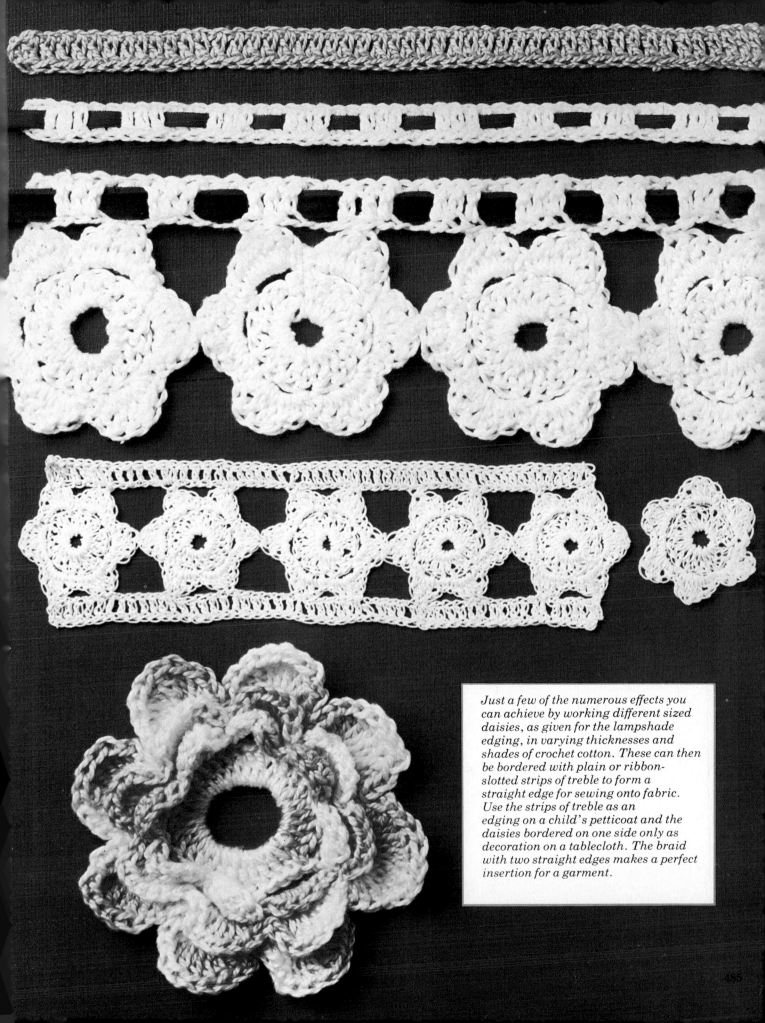

Just a few of the numerous effects you can achieve by working different sized daisies, as given for the lampshade edging, in varying thicknesses and shades of crochet cotton. These can then be bordered with plain or ribbon-slotted strips of treble to form a straight edge for sewing onto fabric. Use the strips of treble as an edging on a child's petticoat and the daisies bordered on one side only as decoration on a tablecloth. The braid with two straight edges makes a perfect insertion for a garment.

Dining chairs– spring and stuff continued

Cloth — upholstery 4

In the last chapter on upholstery a dining chair was fitted with webbing, the springs attached and lashed and the main stuffing inserted and covered. In this chapter the process is completed by stitching the edge, putting in the second stuffing and then finally covering. Your chair is now ready for use.

Stitching the edge

This is done in two stages. The first, which is called blind stitching, pulls enough stuffing to the edges to enable a firm edge to be built up. The second stage, top stitching, forms a roll from this section of stuffing. The roll has to be really firm because the covering fabric is pulled over it, and any unevenness would spoil the shape.

Start the stitching at the back on the left side of chair and work around seat counterclockwise to include back.

To do the blind stitching thread the upholsterer's needle with a good length of twine. Insert the unthreaded end of the needle into the scrim just above the tacks and about 4cm (1½″) from the corner. Insert the needle into the stuffing at an angle of about 45°. It will emerge on the top of the chair about 5cm (2″) in from the edge and 1cm (½″) nearer the corner.

Pull the needle through, stopping as soon as you see the eye, so that it is not completely withdrawn. Push it back into the stuffing again, altering the angle so that it emerges through the side on the same level as where it first entered, but 2.5cm (1″) nearer the corner. You have, in effect, made a V-shaped stitch or loop in the stuffing (fig.1).

Pull the twine through so that there is a tail of about 7.5cm (3″). Tie to main length with a slip knot and pull tight. Insert the needle about 5cm (2″) further along the edge, slanting in the same way as before and bringing it out on the same level on top as the first stitch. Bring it down again at an angle to emerge on the side about 2.5cm (1″) back. Before withdrawing the needle completely, wind the twine hanging in a loop below it, around the needle twice. Pull needle right through.

Put the unthreaded end of the needle into the center of the chair top to anchor it temporarily. Hold the edge of the stuffing with your left hand so that the fingers are on the top and the thumb is on the side. Wrap the twine around your other hand and pull the stitch really tight, pressing down with your left hand at the same time; you should be able to feel the filling being pulled toward the edge.

Continue working around the edge in this way, being careful not to place the twisted section of a stitch so that it has to go around a corner. To finish, knot the twine carefully and tightly.

Correct any unevenness in the stuffing with the regulator, then re-thread the upholsterer's needle with a long length of twine.

Top stitching is similar to blind stitching, the main difference being that the needle is completely pulled through on top of the stuffing so that a stitch can be made on top. This means that the needle should be inserted vertically into the scrim and not inclined to the left as with blind stitching. Starting at a corner, insert the needle about 4cm (1½″) away and about 1cm (½″) above the blind stitching. Push it through so that it emerges on top about 2.5cm (1″) in from the edge.

Re-insert the threaded end of the needle about 2.5cm (1″) to the left of this point, keeping it parallel to the first entry so that it emerges 2.5cm (1″) away (fig.2).

Tie the end of the twine in a slip knot as before. Insert the needle again and complete the stitch, reinserting it about 2.5cm (1″) to the left as before so that it is just short of the first stitch. Before withdrawing the needle completely from the second half of the stitch, wind the twine around it and then pull tight in the same way as for blind stitching. Continue all around

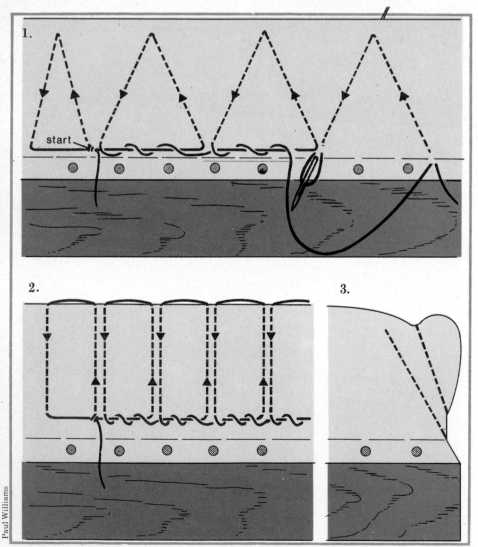

1. The loop made by blind stitches pulls the stuffing to the edge of the seat. *2. Top stitching forms the stuffing into a roll.* *3. A profile of the stitches.*

Paul Williams

the edge in this way. The stitches on top of the chair should form a continuous line, following line of chair.

The second stuffing

Make bridle ties in the scrim as with the first stuffing. Fill the cavity which has been formed by the roll edge with more stuffing tucked under the bridle ties, and cover the chair with a piece of muslin, temporarily tacking this with 10mm (⅜″) fine tacks to the front of the frame, then the back and lastly the sides.

If the original upholstery finished on this face, rather than on the underside of the chair, be careful to place the tacks clear of the line where the wood begins to show. Cut into the muslin at the back corners to fit around the uprights of the chair back, following the method given in Upholstery chapter 2, page 434.

After the muslin has been positioned, tack it in place.

If the front corners of the chair are rounded, make a double pleat or an inverted pleat (as in the photographs), or a single pleat if the corner is square. To keep a smooth line the muslin has to be pulled hard over the roll edges, but be careful to keep the grain of the muslin absolutely straight, putting most of the pressure from back to front, as illustrated, rather than from side to side.

The top cover

Cover the muslin with wadding to prevent the stuffing from working through. Cut a piece of cover fabric on the straight grain large enough to cover the seat in the same style as the original upholstery. Temporarily tack it down with 10mm (⅜″) fine tacks through a single thickness. Finish the corners as for the muslin cover, using the flat end of the regulator to make a smooth finish at the back.

Tack down.

Trim off the excess fabric.

Finishing off. If the cover was attached to the front face of the frame the raw edge and tacks can be hidden with braid, stuck on with a commercial latex adhesive. Miter the braid at the corners and cover the 'works' under the seat with black burlap, using the methods described in Upholstery chapter 2, page 434.

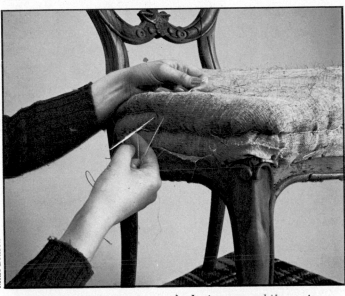

Working top stitching counterclockwise around the seat.

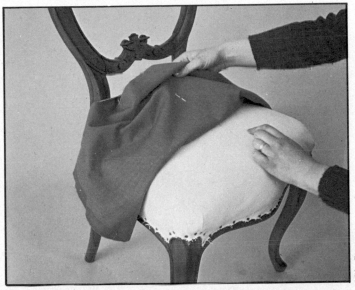

Checking that the grain of the cover fabric is straight.

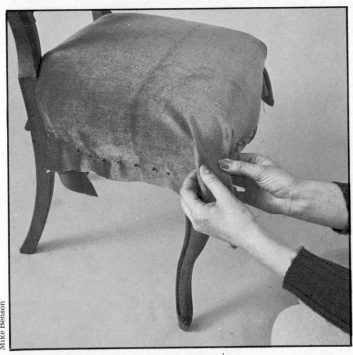

Finishing off the corners in a double pleat.

The re-upholstered chair: elegant and ready for use.

Beginning tie-dyeing

Tie-dyeing is a way of decorating cloth by blocking out certain parts so that they do not 'take' the dye in which the cloth is dipped. This is done by knotting, folding, clipping, tying or binding the cloth so that the dye cannot penetrate these areas. (More complex methods are discussed in the next dyeing chapter.)

Using tie-dye methods, you can create an array of patterns that have an extraordinary illusory quality which is quite unlike anything else that printing or dyeing can produce. By planning which areas of the fabric you want to resist the dye, you can create repeated patterns or position a large motif, such as a flamboyant sunburst, in the center of a garment or any other object.

Tie-dying is an age-old craft which originated in the East, probably in China, and spread along the ancient routes of the silk caravans to many other lands. Medieval Japanese nobles dressed in tie-dyed silks, and in India and Indonesia the craft became a highly developed and refined form of decoration. Examples of tie-dyeing have also been found in Pre-Columbian America, and it is still practiced extensively in Africa where a distinctive style of wonderfully bold patterns has arisen, often using indigo dyes.

What will dye

Any fabric which is not too bulky can be tie-dyed as long as the fiber is receptive to dye. Silk is particularly beautiful when tie-dyed as its floating quality seems to lend itself to the radiant patterns which tie-dye produces. Cotton is perhaps the easiest fabric to work with because it takes dye extremely well and, being comparatively inexpensive, is a good choice for beginners.

Natural fibers (cotton, linen, silk, wool) and man-made rayon can be dyed with commercial cold water dyes. These are *fiber reactive* dyes, which means that the dye molecules form a bond with the fiber, rendering it color fast.

Many synthetic fibers can be dyed with commercial hot water dyes and these come in a wide range of colors and shades. Unfortunately, these dyes are not color fast and must always be washed separately.

Polyesters and fabrics with special finishes—to make them crease or stain-resistant, eg—cannot be dyed. For more details about dyeing different fibers and fiber mixtures, and for using hot and cold water dyes, see Dyeing chapter 1, page 150.

Cloth that is going to be dyed must always be washed first to get rid of any dressing which may have been added by the manufacturer to give it 'body' and finish. Otherwise, the dressing will prevent dye penetrating the cloth.

Tying

Before you begin to tie the cloth it must be dry and free from creases.

It is wise to experiment with a few squares of inexpensive cotton or strips of old sheeting to find out about different effects, to try out different types of string and to see how tightly cloth should be bound.

String. All types of string will prevent penetration of the dye to some degree, but some strings will let dye penetrate more than others. Nylon string is totally resistant to cold water dyes.

Cotton thread is receptive to dyes of all kinds and is therefore not suitable unless your fabric is thickly bunched or folded. With thick bunching you can make graded patterns of color because the inner sections of cloth will receive little or no dye while the outer layers may receive some color through the thread.

Fishing line, plastic cord, rope and linen thread can all be used effectively.

Resist objects of all sorts can be used in tie-dyeing to give interesting and unusual patterns, and you will be able to find many ordinary household items to use. Paper clips, clothes pins, large clips, pipe cleaners—anything that grips the fabric, keeps dye out and is not itself harmed in the dyebath, will work and also will leave its own special mark or pattern.

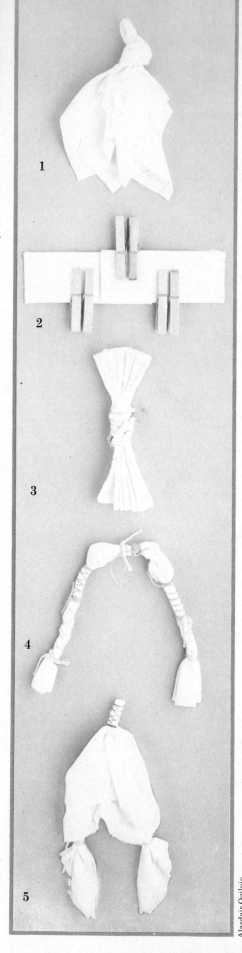

Tie dyeing means binding parts of cloth with cords or other things, like the clothes pins shown, and then dyeing it. The tied-off areas resist the dye and make the patterns. Opposite are some examples of different binding methods and resulting patterns.

Alasdair Ogilvie

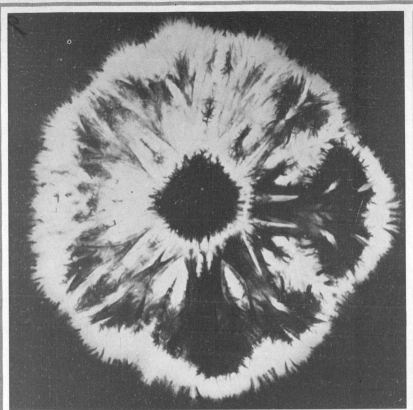

1. *The simplest tie of all is a knot and this can be in the center or on the ends. For a regular effect make the knots equidistant.*

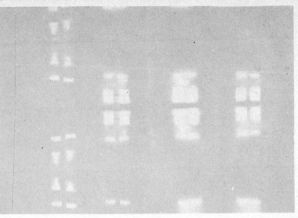

2. *Clothes pins give interesting, blotted effects and cloth should be folded in accordion pleats first for a repeated effect. In the example shown the cloth has been pleated and then folded again in the middle.*

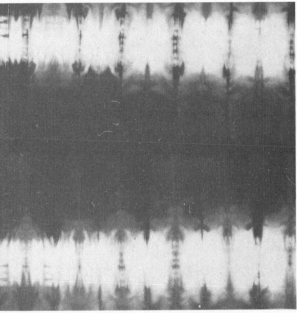

3. *This design is made by folding the piece of cloth in half, accordion pleating it and then binding with strong twine, as shown far left.*

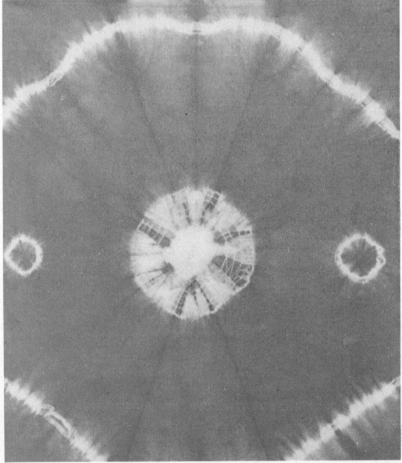

5. *These cobweb-like circles were made by picking up cloth center with a needle, letting it fall in even folds, then binding the center, inverting it and binding again in a lump below.*

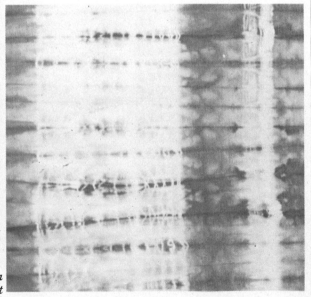

4. *Cloth pleated and tied with spiral ties.*

Steve Bicknell

Rubber bands, wire, dental floss and masking tape are all useful substitutes for string and cord.

Several different objects can be combined to make a pattern on one piece of cloth and this is where your own ingenuity comes in. In the beginning you will have to test the result of each 'tie' before using it as a pattern, but as soon as you become familiar with the effects different 'ties' produce, you can then envisage a pattern and then proceed.

Always consider which 'ties' are most suitable for the type and weight of your material and for the use it will be put to. Fine cottons and silk, for instance, respond to fine threads and a close repetition of delicate ties, while fabrics of a looser weave need a large effect from knotting, pinning or heavy cord.

Repeated patterns should be place-marked with a pencil before tying begins, so that you can be sure of a regular repeat.

All string, thread or cord must be tied very, very tightly and knotted firmly, so that it does not loosen in the dye-bath. If the string is unusually thick, or if for any reason there is a problem in getting the end of the string back to the beginning to make a knot, you can stitch the ends to the rest of the cord by using a large darning needle.

Dyeing

When your 'ties' are all securely tied or fastened, wet the cloth thoroughly and put it into the dyebath for the length of time stated in the manu-facturer's instructions.

When the dye has taken, remove the fabric, leaving the ties intact, and rinse it thoroughly. If you have been using a hot water dye it is advisable to give it a good wash before untying to get rid of any excess dye. Do not undo the ties until the cloth has had time to dry thoroughly, or dye may seep into the white, unprotected areas. When undoing the ties it is very easy to nip the cloth accidentally with your scissors, so be very careful and insert the point of the scissors under the end, not the middle, of the tie.

Special effects can be created with dyes by dipping only part of the cloth into the dye—along the edges of accordion folds, for example.

Another fascinating effect comes from using bleach (Dyeing chapter 4, page 408) on cloth that has been dyed first, and then tied. This is a kind of reverse procedure because it is the dyed areas which make the pattern as the bleach removes the dye from the exposed areas.

By tying cloth with sewing thread or cord that has been dyed with a hot water dye you can make colored lines on fabric where the dye from the cord

seeps through. Although it is much better to experiment on white cloth, you can begin with a light-colored cloth, tie it, and dye a darker shade.

Multi-colored tie-dyeing. Some marvelous color combinations can be made by using more than one dyebath. In this way, the second color can be applied either before or after you undo your first ties. If you make more ties in the same cloth, without untying the first ones, and then put the cloth in a second dyebath, your first ties will result in a white pattern, your second ties will have the color of the first dyebath, and the cloth which was exposed throughout will either be the color of the last dyebath or a blend of both colors.

When working with more than one color it is important to remember that dyes blend. The blending action of dyes presents some exciting possibilities once the basic rules governing dyes and colors are understood. If you tie-dye white cloth light blue, add some more ties and then dye dark blue; in the end you will have white and light blue patterns where the respective ties have been, and the background will be dark blue. But if the second dyebath is yellow, then you will end up with white and light blue patterns on a green background, since the yellow and blue will blend to form green. In multi-colored dyeing, the fabric must be thoroughly rinsed between each dyeing, and if the first ties are to be untied then the cloth must be allowed to dry thoroughly first.

Silk scarf was tied once and dyed yellow, then more ties were made.

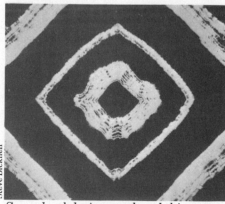

Second red dyeing produced this pattern

Cotton sheets and pillow cases wer
crumpled into sausages, tied at rando
and dyed in a washing machin

Stripping, filling and bleaching

A lot of old furniture has been badly treated over the years although structurally it may still be in good condition. Congealed and dirty paint, damaged varnish, delicate details obscured by layers and layers of one finish or another—all require to be stripped and made good. Dents, scratches, cracks and holes must be filled in and, if the wood has become discolored, it may need bleaching.

Solid wood, such as pine, oak or beech, responds well to stripping. If, however, your wood is veneered or is delicately made, be careful about stripping it completely, as some solvents (including water) may swell the wood and loosen the glue, causing the whole thing to fall apart.

Stripping polish

Wax polish and oily surfaces. Rub over with turpentine (or turpentine substitute) and fine steel wool, then immediately mop with an absorbent rag. Repeat the cycle until you reach bare wood.

French polish can easily be removed with denatured alcohol. Wipe it on generously and leave it for a few minutes. When the polish is softened, take it off with a cabinet scraper, then with fine steel wool moistened with more denatured alcohol. Leave it to dry and finish with sandpaper.

Small areas of damaged French polish can be removed using a commercial varnish remover or very strong ammonia.

Stripping lacquer and old varnish

Lacquer means the black or dark red lacquer found on Oriental furniture, and not the glass paint sometimes described as lacquer. Most lacquered articles (though not all) are old, and consequently quite valuable and unsuitable for stripping and re-painting.

Old varnish means the old-fashioned, thick, brownish varnish found on furniture over thirty years old. This is made of resins dissolved in oils and solvents, and is completely different from cellulose, polyurethane and melamine varnishes.

Cabinet Scraper. The cleanest way to remove oil-based varnish and lacquer is with a cabinet scraper. This is a tool which is also used for finishing new wood before painting it. The cabinet scraper you need does not have a handle. You can also use a skarsten for removing varnish. It is a piece of sheet steel about 100mm x 50mm (4"x2") and 1.6mm ($\frac{1}{16}$") thick. It is held by curling the fingers around the ends and pressing the middle away from you

Make an attractive piece of furniture by stripping off the old finish.

with the thumbs so that the steel is bent in a shallow curve. The edge is then applied to the wood. Tilt the scraper away from you and push it along the grain, always working away from your body. Never use it across the grain.

A scraper is sharpened by filing the edge to remove the blunt burr (i.e. rounded edge). The edge is sharpened on a fine oilstone, and then turned over with the shank of a screwdriver as shown in fig.1.

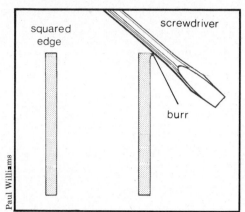

1. *How to sharpen a cabinet scraper.*

Holes and corners. For hole and corner work use an old (but sharp) chisel. Alternatively, scrape moldings and curves with a suitably-shaped piece of broken glass. Smash a thick bottle and keep all the large pieces; you are bound to find one with the right angles on it. Use rubber gloves to hold the glass, or wrap tape around the top.

Cellulose varnishes and lacquers

To remove cellulose-based varnishes and lacquers use a commercial stripper or acetone, cellulose thinners, ammonia, caustic soda or turpentine. You may have to test small areas first to find the right solvent. It is wise to make your tests on unnoticeable areas. Stand the object on sheets of newspaper and, if it has legs, put them in bowls to collect drips. Swab the surface with the solvent and carefully use a scraper for reaching into difficult corners. There is no need to remove more than the damaged area of the finish, or perhaps the section containing it, unless the whole piece has deteriorated badly, is scratched all over, cracked into thousands of little cracks, or badly bloomed to a widespread milky opacity.

Caustic soda. One way of stripping off the finish on an old piece of solid furniture is to take it outdoors and swab it continuously with caustic soda. Use one can of crystals and add it to a liter (2pt) of water—not vice versa or the mixture will spit.

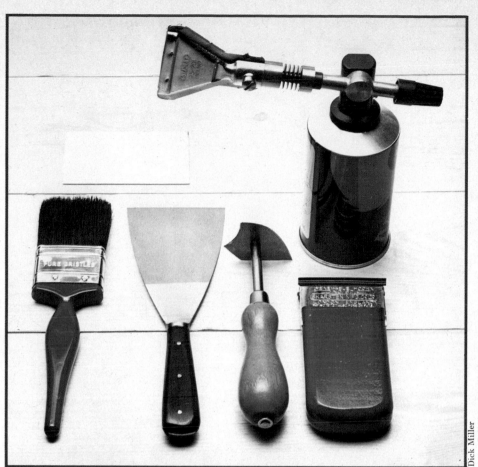

Wear a smock, rubber gloves and approved safety glasses, and use a mop of some kind to apply the solution. The varnish or paint will soften and swab right off. Finish the job by sluicing the piece down with clean water and a little vinegar to neutralize the caustic soda. This treatment will darken the wood. It is a drastic method of stripping, so be sure your furniture is solid wood and not veneer which will warp and probably disintegrate.

Ammonia. Some old paints (which in themselves may add to the value of the furniture) can be removed only with a straight solution of ammonia. Again, this will darken the wood.

Modern varnishes. Varnished furniture less than thirty years old is normally covered in cellulose, plastic or polyurethane varnish. Polyurethane is very hardwearing and widely used. These varnishes do not need to be removed unless you find them very ugly or they are heavily damaged or so thick that moldings are clogged up. If you do have to remove them, use paint stripper.

Veneers

Many pieces of old or second-hand furniture are entirely surfaced with sheets of polished veneer. A careful look at the end grain along the vertical edge of a flat surface will usually reveal enough of a difference in the grains to show up the veneer.

Stripping tools. Top: cabinet scraper (left) and blowlamp (right). Bottom (left to right): paint brush, stripping knife, multi-purpose shavehook, double-bladed scraper.

When you are stripping veneer of varnish or lacquer it is essential to remember that old veneers are very thin and have been fixed with animal glue, so great care must be taken not to let water or other solvents soak into the wood. If water gets under the veneer it will lift and you will have a major restoration job.

Veneers or marquetry inlays were never varnished with anything containing turpentine or its substitutes, as these would have softened the glue. Quick-drying, volatile spirit varnishes were used instead.

New veneers are used with stronger glue. Even so, you should be careful not to soak the furniture or to lift the glue with strong solvents.

Stripping paint

If the old paint is rough and pitted but soundly adhered to the base, a fine commercial filler (spackle), will make it good. If the surface is badly damaged, the paint should be stripped off completely as there is no alternative method of obtaining a good, final finish. This can be done in one of three ways: mechanical, by heat, or by using the chemical method.

493

Mechanical stripping
You will need:
Double-bladed scraper.
For small damaged areas use a double-bladed scraper. Use the serrated edge to score the paint film, and shave off the paint surface with the other blade, using the scraper like a plane.

Chemical stripping
You will need:
Chemical paint stripper.
Old 5cm (2″) brush for applying stripper.
Larger-sized, stiff-bristled brush to work stripper into crevices (wire wool will do instead).
Multi-purpose shavehook for scraping paint. Shavehooks are also available in various sizes for scraping areas difficult to reach.
Bowl of water, vinegar and a rag to neutralize chemical splashes.
Rubber gloves and goggles to protect eyes and hands.
Asbestos sheet or thick layer of newspaper to protect the floor.
Container (not plastic) for the paint scraps.

This type of stripper, available as a liquid or jelly, is suitable for intricately molded surfaces, beaded areas and surfaces close to glass. Ask your retailer's advice on a particular stripper for a particular job.
Using an old brush, carefully apply the stripper in small sections to the painted surface, working it well into crevices and cracks. Leave the chemical to soften and 'lift' the paint. Scrape it off with a multi-purpose shavehook or edge scraper when the treated area bubbles and curls. The paint scraps are extremely caustic and should be burned immediately or, alternatively, wrapped in newspaper and put in the garbage, out of reach of children and animals. Strippers rarely take off paint in a complete strip but tend to shrivel the thin, top layer. Several successive applications may be needed.
Wear old clothes and gloves for this work as a protection against chemical splashes and skin burns because most strippers are caustic. Protect eyes, if necessary, by wearing goggles, and work outside or leave windows open to prevent the build-up of fumes. If you

Various ways of stripping wood. Top left: lift old varnish and lacquer with a cabinet scraper. Top right: a double-bladed scraper is convenient for small areas. Center chemical stripper softens and loosens paint and varnish before scraping it off. Bottom left: the flame size of a blowlamp can be adjusted for melting the paint. Don't burn the wood. Bottom right: quickly lift off the shriveled paint with a broad stripping knife.

get stripper on your skin wash off immediately with lots of water.

When the wood is stripped clean, wash it down with turpentine substitute. Work it well into the surface with a fine grade steel wool, and when it evaporates go over the surface with sandpaper. This removes all traces of the stripper and prevents any residue from reacting with the new paint.

Heat stripping

You will need:
'Handyman' blowtorch. (The experienced can use a commercial gas or butane blowtorch.)
Broad stripping knife, 7mm (3″).
Asbestos sheet to protect the floor.
Container (not plastic) for the paint scraps.
You will also find turpentine substitute useful for cleaning surfaces, and medium sandpaper useful for keying clean surfaces.

This is the quickest way of stripping paint. The heat is applied with a blowtorch. Different fittings are available ranging from pin-point flame to a fan spread for large areas. Choose the most appropriate fitting for your surface.

Always treat your blowtorch with great respect, and use a sheet of asbestos, not newspaper or a drop cloth, to protect the floor from hot paint strippings. If you are using it for the first time practice on a flat surface first. For difficult areas, like moldings and around mirrors, it is advisable to use a chemical stripper, as the glass can be cracked by the heat of the blowtorch, particularly if the flame is too large or kept stationary.

Play the flame backward and forward across the surface to melt the paint, but leave the under surface intact. As the paint shrivels, scrape it with the broad scraper, held at an angle (this prevents the melted paint from falling on your hands). Put the paint scraps into the waste container.

Get into the habit of turning the blowtorch flame away from the surface while you are scraping—this helps to prevent accidental surface burns and avoids setting the paint afire.

Filling holes and cracks

Restore the surface of painted furniture by cleaning out blemishes to the raw wood surface and then refilling the gaps with plastic wood or a commercial non-shrinking stopper. Rub level with fine sandpaper.

Holes (over keyhole size) should be filled in by cutting a matching wood block to shape. Make sure that the grain of the wood runs the same way. Glue the wood block with urea formaldehyde glue, then plane it flush with the surface.

Bleaching

The main reasons for bleaching wood are to lighten the overall color or to remove local staining, but you may not need to bleach at all. A degree of shade differences and natural variation in color can be quite natural and harmonious.

Ordinary domestic bleach is very dilute, too mild for drastic work on wood. Stronger mixtures can be made with crystals, but be careful to add crystals to water, not water to crystals —the heat generated can cause a small quantity of water to spit and boil. Obtain commercial wood bleaches wherever possible.

Sodium hypochlorite is good at removing color from wood but choose oxalic acid for ink or iron stains— about 100gm (3½oz) to a liter (2pt) of water if you buy it in crystal form.

Like most bleaches it is *very poisonous*. Two-part bleaches are the most powerful of all and, if not carefully watched, can attack Scotch glue used for veneers.

Be sure to read the manufacturer's instructions for all bleaches. These instructions will also tell you how long to leave the bleach on the wood.

Finishing

Stripping and bleaching can raise the surface of the wood, especially if it is softwood, so you should rub along the grain with medium sandpaper when it is dry. The wood will be ready for oiling, staining, varnishing or painting, as described in Finishes chapter 1, page 72, and chapter 2, page 404.

This chest of drawers has responded well to careful stripping.

Sgraffito and stencils

After firing single-colored enamels you will now be familiar with the actual firing technique and counter-enameling (see Enamel chapter 2, page 190). However, if you start to combine different colors and do a few experiments you will come up with varying results.

For example, if you powder a blank thinly with one color, say blue, and then powder it with yellow, the end result is not green, as you might expect, but a speckled combination of the two colors. Alternatively, if you fire one color first and then fire another color on top of it, the top color, depending on the firing time, would dominate, showing specks of the initial color used.

These color combinations can be very interesting, especially if you use different tones of the same color, eg a turquoise blue on a midnight blue.

However, there are definite ways to control the color combinations to give you the designs and colors you want, rather than just haphazard results.

You can continue to make small enamel pieces for jewelry or buttons and if you want something larger, as a sampler, you can make a number of small square or oblong enamels and glue them together on a base, perhaps to make a large table mat.

To apply the techniques described you will need the equipment and tools mentioned in Enamel chapter 1, page 106, and you will also need a stilt or tripod for counter-enameling.

Sgrafitto

Sgrafitto is an Italian word meaning 'scratched'. In enameling, the technique of sgrafitto produces a pattern or design by scratching in the enamel powder, before the firing, to show another color underneath.

You can experiment with opaque and transparent enamel powders, but generally opaque enamels give more satisfactory results because they show stronger contrast and combination of colors.

It is possible to do extremely fine and intricate designs with sgrafitto, but you need a steady hand and patience for it.

If you have some enamels from previous firings that are not satisfactory, you can practice with these because it is possible to overcome imperfections on the surface by firing another layer of enamel on top of it.

The first color will eventually form the lines of the pattern and the second color will be the surrounding area forming the bulk of the color. So choose your enamels with this in mind. You can make abstract designs with simple lines or, if you are good at drawing, you can make almost any other pattern or outline you like.

To rectify an imperfectly fired piece decide on the color you want to use and powder it, making it slightly thicker where the faults occur.

Use a sieve for this, or attach a clean piece of muslin, by means of a rubber band, over the top of an open jar and use the powder direct from the jar.

Take any pointed tool, the end of a water color brush or a match-stick will do, and draw the design. The first coat of enamel must show so, to begin with, do not make these lines too fine. Make sure that the lines are of even width, if that is the effect you want, and also make sure that all the powder is cleaned off the lines.

Fire the enamel. Watch it closely because you must remove it from the kiln as soon as it is fired and before the enamel begins to flow. If you over-fire the enamel it will flow, breaking the lines and making the enamel flat.

If you start with a new blank clean it by rubbing it with emery paper. Counter-enamel the piece.

Clean off the firescale. Apply the base coat of the design and fire.

Apply the second color to the base color and draw your design.

Fire the piece on the stilt, watch it carefully, and remove when fired.

Sgrafitto—Sifting powder onto an enameled surface.

Drawing the design in the powder with the end of a brush.

Dick Miller

An old Japanese stencil was used by Ken Hammond for this piece. Each rectangle was fired individually.

Stencil—Positioning stencil on an enameled surface.

Sifting powder evenly onto the cut-out area.

Removing the stencil with very great care.

Using a paint brush to remove powder outside stencil area.

Dick Miller

Stencils

To create solid areas of color rather than simply patterns created with lines you need to use a stencil.

Make a stencil from cardboard which is stiff but not thick. A utility or trimming knife is useful for cutting the stencil, especially for intricate work. Cut the desired shape from a piece of cardboard slightly larger than the blank you are using. Start with fairly simple shapes such as a square, circle or heart shape.

Counter-enamel the piece.

Fire the blank with the first color.

Place stencil on the side fired top-side and powder the cut-out area evenly. You can use either the cut-out stencil or the cardboard surrounding the cut-out area. Whichever you use make sure the edges are neat and smooth.

Remove the stencil carefully and, should there be any powder outside the area of the stencil, use a small soft brush to remove it.

Fire the piece again and remove it as soon as it is ready. If you over-fire it the enamel will flow, breaking the lines you want.

There are many variations to the above

techniques. You can combine stenciling with sgrafitto or you can use more than one stencil and a number of colors.

Each color and stencil will require firing.

You need not be limited to cut-out stencils. Use any dried leaf or fern which lies flat and place it on the enamel to give you an outline. You will find that tweezers are useful for removing the delicate stencil motif and you can then use a pointed tool to tidy up any fine lines that are not clear enough.

A group of enameled pieces show sgraffito and stenciling techniques. Designers Pheobe Douglas and Betty Groocock.

General hints

Red enamels are slightly more difficult to perfect as they tend to burn when over-fired. Remove them from the kiln as soon as they are fired.

Yellows are also fairly difficult to fire but most other colors are hard-firing and will withstand a number of firings.

Pitted surface and black patches. If these are formed it is because the enamel has been applied unevenly, and too thinly. This can be corrected by applying another layer of enamel, making it slightly thicker where the imperfections occur, and re-firing it.

Uneven enamel, without any signs of burns, means that the enamel is underfired and should be returned to the kiln.

Store enamels in airtight containers. If the enamel is damp it will lift from the metal during firing. If the enamel contains any dust this will make holes in the fired enamel. Keep your working area as clean as possible and you will find that cleanliness will prevent most of the things that could go wrong. So, remember this when removing firescale and do it away from your powders.

Re-using blanks. Enamels which are quite beyond repair are still not a com-plete waste. You can place the enamel between a fold of cloth and hit it with a hammer to shatter the enamel and salvage the metal blank for re-use.

Polishing the edges. The edge of the enamels will be slightly black where the copper has formed firescale. You can remove this by carefully rubbing it down with a carborundum stone. It is a delicate procedure because you could damage or chip the enamel. However, it does improve the appearance of your work if you can show the copper edge of the blank rather than a black firescale edge, so it's worth the effort.

Japanese flower arrangements

The contemplation of beauty has long been an essential element in the culture of Japan and the art of Ikebana arises out of it. The very simplicity of Ikebana arrangements is partly to allow the contemplation of each flower, branch and leaf, and a mass of flowers and foliage would be spiritually indigestible to the Japanese.

Ikebana means, quite literally, 'living flowers' but over the centuries it has

Japanese flower arrangements involve the use of three basic stems which represent Man, Heaven and Earth. Those shown here are by Stella Coe.

Dick Miller

come to refer to a way of arranging them using an exciting dimension altogether missing in Western-style flower arrangements. In Ikebana it is not just visual beauty that is important but also beauty of expression. Flowers, grasses, reeds, and shrubs all have their own symbolic meanings and by using this 'language of plants' within the basic laws of Ikebana it is possible to express mood and personal philosophy in flower arrangements just as in poetry and literature.

Ikebana has become increasingly popular in the West and goes particularly well with modern furniture.

History of Ikebana

The art of flower arranging in Japan goes back to the 6th century when the Buddhist religion was introduced from China and with it the ritual of offering flowers to the Buddha, usually in great bronze vessels.

By the 10th century a school had been founded to teach these ritual arrangements, based on keeping the lines and shapes of nature and observing the intrinsic harmony of the universe. The early arrangements, called Rikka, were huge, up to 4.5m (15′) tall, and very formal in appearance; but although they became much altered with time, the basic premises regarding the harmony and balance of nature remained in Ikebana as in Buddhism.

The practice of offering flowers to the Buddha soon spread from the temple to the homes of nobles and dignitaries and, of necessity, the style of arrangements became simplified and smaller in size so as to occupy the Tokonoma, the alcove sacred to Buddha in the Japanese household.

Eventually other adaptations were also made but none were more significant than those in the mid-19th century. For the first time flower arranging became a female occupation as well as a male one and it was soon an expected accomplishment in any young woman. At this time also, a new style developed, called Moribana, which used shallow containers, thereby giving more freedom in arrangements. For the first time Ikebana moved out of the traditional alcove or Tokonoma and into the three-dimensional environment of the home, thus further broadening the scope for creating designs. Before this, arrangements had been visible from only one angle, now they could be contemplated from all around and from above. Moribana is still one of the most popular styles of Ikebana.

Symbolism

In order to 'speak' with flowers it is necessary to know what the symbols mean and although it would take some time to learn the complete Japanese

Moribana is a style of arrangement which uses a low container.

Alan Duns

flower vocabulary we can automatically understand a great many.

Poets have always drawn metaphors from nature, and in much the same way Ikebana uses the actual material of nature to make a poetic statement. As Shakespeare, for example, describes oncoming age or death as a time 'When yellow leaves, or none, or few, do hang Upon those boughs', so the Japanese flower arranger might express the same sentiment by actually putting branches on which only a few leaves remain into a container.

There are, in Ikebana, three basic symbols on which all arrangements are built and every 'story' told. Ikebana arrangements are made up of three main stems which respectively symbolize Heaven, Man and Earth. Other stems have a supporting role only (and there are special instances where 'Man' is removed and only two stems make up an arrangement).

Against this universal stage, expressions of all moods and outlooks are possible by the addition of not just flowers but many other natural materials—branches, grasses, rocks, driftwood, shells. All have their special meanings and many are universally familiar: the delicate peach blossom represents womanly beauty and modesty, the upright iris stands for bravery, and the lotus—one of the earliest flowers associated with Buddha—denotes nobility and sincerity. On the whole, grasses tend to be masculine, blossoms feminine.

Just as important are the seasonal symbols. Autumnal leaves and torn leaves convey decline, sadness. Tight

buds, half-opened ones and full-blown flowers show the time of future, present and past. The correct seasonal content of an arrangement is also important in Japan and no flower or plant is put into an arrangement that is not naturally in season. This is less important in Western countries, however, since the difference between indoors and out is more pronounced.

Making arrangements

Although several styles of arrangements are being taught today in some 2000 Ikebana schools in Japan alone, the best-known and most widely used styles are the Moribana, which uses a shallow container, and the Nageire (see page 503), dating from an earlier time, which uses a tall container. The same basic principles apply to both.

In both Moribana and Nageire the 3 symbolic stems, Heaven, Man and Earth can be arranged in one of two styles—upright or slanting—to make natural-looking designs. In the upright, Heaven is always the highest stem, then Man, then Earth. But in the slanting style, man is exalted and placed at a higher angle than Heaven. Other materials keep the same relationship as found in nature: a tree branch is never placed lower than a flower and grasses never higher than a tree. The length of each stem is governed by certain laws as is the angle the stems are arranged at.

In keeping with the requirement for simplicity, no more than three different types of materials are used in any one arrangement and uneven numbers of flowers are considered more aesthetic as well as being lucky. The latter is often disregarded in Western Ikebana since flowers are often sold in even numbers and even the most sincere Ikebana master, being Buddhist and believing all plant life to be sacred, would not condone the waste of a flower which has already been cut.

Basic equipment

The success of an arrangement depends very much on the proper container and the securing of the plants.

Containers are an integral part of the arrangement and should blend as much as possible with it. Earthy tones of green, gray or beige are safe to start with. Texture is also important and china, pottery, metalware or wood can all be used, depending on the statement being made.

For Moribana the container must be shallow and flat, but deep enough to hold two or three inches of water. Nageire is, of course, much taller, but in both types the height of the arrangement will be determined by the diameter of the lip of the container.

The Japanese normally use a small wooden stand, *dai*, to support the container on a table but this is often dispensed with in the west.

A pinholder or kenzan (fig.1a) is needed, especially in shallow Moribana arrangements. Heavy branches can be secured by diagonal cuts to fit into the kenzan along with flowers and other materials (fig.1b). If a stem is particularly weighty then one kenzan can be placed upside down on the side of the other to balance it (fig.1c).

Kenzans should never be glued to containers since minute adjustments are usually required up to the last minute. Moreover, kenzans are never placed in the center of a Moribana container as this would appear too carefully planned and 'unnatural'. In tall arrangements wire mesh is sometimes used or a counterbalance system (fig.2) using a separate stick as an anchor. Florists' foam is also useful for embedding tall plants in vases.

In Ikebana, proper flower scissors with serrated edges are a great asset and a sharp knife is also helpful to cut through or whittle down thick wooden stems. You will also need a protractor for measuring angles.

Moribana

These arrangements are both attractive to look at and easy for beginners. They look best on a low table which is free from other distracting objects, and the background should be as simple as possible.

Suggested combinations. Beech branches and daffodils. Tree ivy and tulips. Pussy willow and jonquils.

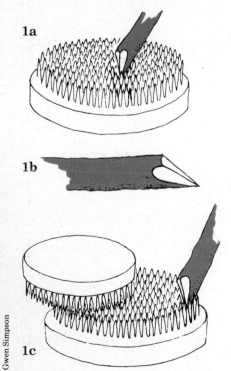

1. *A kenzan or pinholder is used in many arrangements to hold materials.*

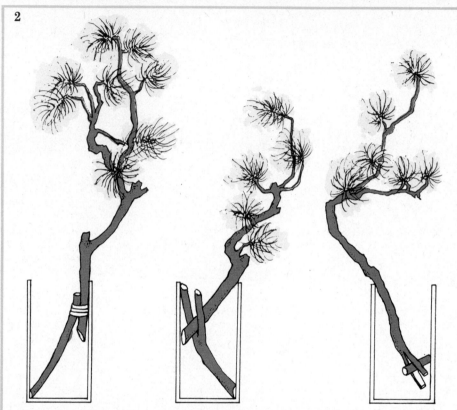

2. *Getting the right angle is a special problem in tall arrangements, but various methods of balancing and counterbalancing can be employed.*

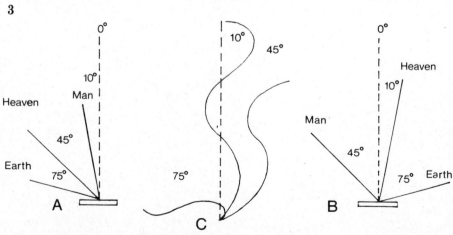

3. *In slanting arrangements (a) 'Man' is higher than 'Heaven' and 'Earth', while in upright arrangments (b) 'Heaven' is higher than 'Man'. Each stem must measure exactly the angles indicated. The distance between the tops of each stem must be consistent with the degree of angle indicated (c).*

Select an appropriate container and a kenzan which will be heavy enough to secure your arrangement.

Cutting the stems. Measure the width of your container and the depth. In a standard arrangement 'Heaven' will be equivalent in stem-length to the width of the container plus the depth and up to half as much again (depending on personal choice).

'Man' is three-quarters of the length of 'Heaven' and 'Earth' is three-quarters as long as 'Man'.

Supporting stems or fillers are never as long as the main stem and should be different lengths from each other.

Remove any unwanted leaves and trim branches to suit the curve you want to make. Branches can often be bent to emphasize a curve by carefully bending and twisting at the same time.

Angles are measured from upright zero as shown in fig.3, and those used are the constant angles of 10°, 45° and 75°. The distance between the tips of the stems should be consistent with the degree of angle required (fig. 3c).

In Moribana the kenzan must always be invisible at a distance of a meter (yard) from the arrangement. This must often be done by using camouflage such as leaves, moss, pebbles.

In slanting arrangements a windswept look is achieved. 'Man' stands above 'Heaven' and 'Earth', eg 'Man' is at an angle of 10° from vertical zero (fig.3a), 'Heaven' is 45° and 'Earth' is 75°.

In upright arrangements 'Heaven' is at an angle of 10° and 'Man' is 45° (a reversal of the above). In both, 'Earth' is 75° from vertical zero (fig. 3b).

Placement of the stems in the rear, side or foreground of arrangements varies.

Nageire

Basically, Nageire is like Moribana but it is a bit more difficult to work arrangements in a tall container. The results, however, are worth it and are perhaps the best suited of all Ikebana styles to Western interiors.

Suggested combinations. Oak branches and roses or jonquils. Bare branches with chrysanthemums. Willow branches with tulips.

In Nageire, special balancing techniques must often be used to get an asymmetrical effect (fig.2).

The length of the stems is determined, as in Moribana, by measuring the diameter of the top of the container and its depth and adding the two together. This gives the length of the 'Heaven' stem. For extra height it is possible to add up to half as much

again but you must also allow for the amount of stem which will be submerged in the vase and the length of this will depend on your method of fixing.

In Nageire, larger flowers can be used than in the more delicate Moribana, because of the height of the container. In either, a splendid scope exists for poetic and decorative expression.

Nageire arrangements are characterized by tall containers. In this one two stems are pine, the third is rose.

Neutral color schemes

Brilliant color may dazzle and delight us but subtle, natural, neutral colors can have an equal charm—both as a background and foil to brighter hues and also in their own right. Brown, gray, cream, beige, eau-de-nil and sand, string, putty and bone kinds of colors can be very varied and full of nuances—even though they may appear to be almost colorless.

Even gradations of gray, from black to white, can be most effective and flattering for clothes—eyes, skin and hair can stand out without distracting competition. In this way simple color highlights shape and texture, light and shade, especially when neutral tones are used.

These are the colors of nature and of man-made things which have been worn and washed and weathered by the elements. For this reason they have a restful, eternal quality which satisfies. Collect seed heads and look carefully at their colors. Notice how much variation there is in shape and texture: the blue-white of honesty pods against the cream of thistle and artichoke; the smooth copper-brown of beech leaves against speckly dock spikes of the same color. There are also the natural colors of leather, basketwork, of undyed wool and the earth color glazes in pottery.

Weaving experiment. If you have some thick neutral colored yarns or worn-out panty hose cut into strips, try making some tiny woven samples.

You will need:
A small piece of thickish cardboard about 5cm x 10cm (2"x 4").
A big needle or bodkin.
Thin black or gray darning yarn.
Ruler and pencil. Old scissors.
A collection of soft fibers (thick yarn or stockings), in browns and grays.

1. *Cut notches along the short edges.*

Method. Mark along the short sides of the cardboard every 6mm (¼"). Cut out a V at every mark (fig.1) about 6mm (¼") deep to make a row of points. Tie the darning yarn around the top first point. Keep the yarn on top and bring it down to wind under the bottom second point. Bring it up around the top third point and so on until the cardboard is covered. This is like a tiny loom with the warp threads ready for weaving. Thread up your bodkin and start to weave.

Try putting close colors together and gradating them from dark to light; then try putting the darkest color next to the lightest. With close shades of one color copy the colors in a seed head. You can make a circle of cardboard and weave a circular representation of a thistle head, for example, with its warm golden center and blue-gray encircling calyx (fig.2).

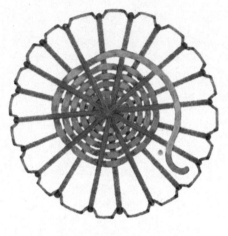

Victoria Drew

2. *A threaded cardboard circle.*

In another experiment you might like to use one neutral color only in various thicknesses and invent varieties of weaving patterns, over and under different numbers of threads—this will show how texture and thickness affects color.

Contrast. Just as neutral color combinations abound in nature so there are as many examples of bright color set against a neutral background—cactus flowers against desert sand, or hawthorn berries against autumn browns. Each of these is an example of contrast of hues and of tones.

Experiment. Select from a color magazine areas of neutral color and of bright contrast. Cut up into 2.5cm (1") or 4cm (1½") squares without fussing about the exact measurements. Arrange together on a dark background so that the edges touch or slightly overlap. Stick down. Repeat the experiment with a different color scheme and different width stripes. These experiments in neutral colors could form the basis for many crafts—crochet, patchwork, weaving, collage.

Peter Heinz

Necklace of date stones, coffee beans, seeds and bone segments. Designed by Mary Seyd.

Creative ideas 18

Bold brass belts

Brass door hinges lead a double life. They are used here to make a strong, bold belt fastening.

You must be sure to use a hinge that has a loose pin, that is, one where the pin which holds the two halves of the hinge together is removable.

You will need:

One loose pin brass hinge 7.5cm (3″) deep.

Strip of buckram 7cm (2$\frac{7}{8}$″) wide, cut a little longer than your waist (or hip) measurement to allow for adjustment when finishing.

Length of fabric cut to same length as buckram and 14cm (5$\frac{1}{2}$″) wide (a corded furnishing fabric is ideal). This forms the edging and lining.

1.14m (1$\frac{1}{4}$yd) webbing or braid, 5cm (2″) wide.

6 wooden beads that will fit the holes left for the screws on the hinge.

Strong thread.

Needle.

Making-up. Buckram is usually rolled so that there is an inner and outer curve to the piece. Make the inner curve form the inside of the belt.

Be sure that the buckram is accurately cut and that the fabric is cut on exactly the straight of grain.

☐ Center and lay the inner curved side of the buckram on the wrong side of fabric strip and trim to within 1.5cm (½″) from each end to allow for neatening. Fold over ends to neaten.

☐ Fold fabric overlap to right side of buckram and machine stitch 5mm (¼″) away from each edge through all layers using a long stitch and heavy needle (fig.1).

☐ On the right side, center the webbing over the raw edges, stitching down center and each edge to hold firm. Make two more rows of stitching as shown in diagram. Always stitch in one direction only, not backward and forward, to avoid puckering.

By sewing beads into the screw holes, attach one half of hinge to the neatened edge, placing the end against the hinge pin holes (fig.2). If you find webbing and hinge of the same width, you can attach the hinge directly to the webbing, without the bother of lining it.

Below. A fashionable belt with a simple brass hinge buckle.

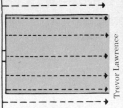

1. Stitching lines.

2. Attaching hinge.

Above. A dismantled loose pin hinge.

Making round and oval boxes

To make round boxes

With a compass, carefully draw a circle on cardboard to make the bottom of the box.

With the same center draw another circle with a radius 1.3cm (½″) wider than the first one.

Cut a straight piece of cardboard the length of the circumference of the inner circle, plus a 1.3cm (½″) overlap, and the height you want the box to be.

Overlap the sides and stick them together to make a cylinder.

To make a base. If using thick cardboard, score on the dotted inner line of the base circle and cut on the solid outer line as shown in fig.1.

Snip into the outer circle and remove alternate segments to make tabs as shown. Bend tabs upward and stick to the base of the cylinder with the tabs inside the body of the box.

1

2

1,2. Cut out segments if cardboard base is thick, or V-notches if it is thin. Then bend up tabs and glue to attach base to insides of box.

If using thinner cardboard, the base can be V-notched (fig.2).

Make the lid the same way as the base, but draw the inner circle 1.5mm ($\frac{1}{16}$") wider in radius. Make the side of the lid about 1.3cm ($\frac{1}{2}$") deep.

Covering round boxes

Wallpaper is suitable for covering round boxes. It comes in hundreds of attractive designs and colors and will also add strength to the box. But wallpaper will not bend sharply and should therefore be butted at the side joins and cut right up to the top and bottom edges of the box.

Most thinner paper will bend easily, so when using them cut a circle of paper the same size as the box base with an additional 1.3cm ($\frac{1}{2}$") margin all around. Cut tabs 1.3cm ($\frac{1}{2}$") into the circle, stick the circle to the bottom of the box, then turn up the overlapping tabs and stick them all around the sides of the box.

Cut a strip of paper the length of the circumference of the box with a 1.3cm ($\frac{1}{2}$") overlap. For the depth you can add an extra 1.3cm ($\frac{1}{2}$") for turning over the top edge to the inside of the box or you can cut it to the top of the box only. Stick around the sides of the box covering the turned-up tabs of the base.

Oval boxes

Make these in the same way as round boxes. Either draw around an oval

It's a pretty idea to make your own hatbox or cover an old one with wallpaper to match your bedroom walls.

An old shop-bought oval box is covered with floral paper to hide the manufacturer's name. But floral paper stops just short of the edges of the box to allow original gilt to decorate the rims.

shape to obtain a pattern, or see Design know-how, Chapter 8, page 224, for instructions on how to draw ovals.

Lining boxes

Boxes can be given an inner cardboard lining to make a recessed base and to make a stronger box.

Make up the outer cylinder as before, but do not add the base yet.

Cut lining cardboard 6mm ($\frac{1}{4}$") shorter and 3mm ($\frac{1}{8}$") narrower than outer cylinder. Bend into a cylinder, stick and then slide it inside the outer box, leaving 6mm ($\frac{1}{4}$") at the bottom (fig.3). Cut base circle of cardboard the same diameter as outer shell. Push this base circle up into the outer cylinder until it is stopped by the lining cylinder. Hold the base circle in place by sticking a circular lining rim of cardboard 6mm ($\frac{1}{4}$") deep inside outer cylinder. The base is now firmly sandwiched between the lining cylinder and the lining rim.

3

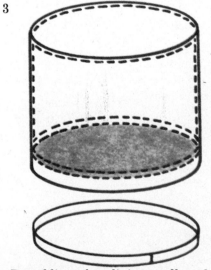

Victoria Drew

3. Dotted lines show lining cardboard used to make a stronger box. Lining rim is the same diameter as the base.

Casting from incised surfaces

Plaster of Paris is an ideal material for making casts as you can see from reading the previous chapters which dealt with rubber molds and impressing with plaster stamps.

The rubber mold method is not, however, the only way in which plaster casts can be made. This chapter covers an interesting technique for making exact replicas of a variety of incised surfaces.

Just think of the enormous number of attractive and unusual incised surfaces around you which are so familiar that you hardly stop to notice them. Look out for Victorian and Edwardian cast-iron work on plaques, recreation park signs, memorials, manhole covers, lettering in stonework and interesting inscriptions or epitaphs on tombstones. All these incised surfaces can, with care, be cast in plaster of Paris.

The process works by rubbing a piece of kitchen foil (or heavier duty foil if you can find it) over the incised surface. A plaster cast can then be made from the template formed in this way. The relief should be fairly low, or the foil will tear when it is rubbed into the crevices. Many surfaces are excellent for rubbing, but never under any circumstance should you work on brass or crumbling stone. Any piece of grit trapped beneath the foil will scratch brass and cause further erosion to weakened stone.

To cast from an incised surface
You will need:
Aluminum foil, preferably heavy duty.
Stiff nylon brush.
Masking tape.
Flat board larger than the area to be rubbed.
Plaster of Paris.
4 thick pieces of wood to frame the cast.
Aerosol shaving foam.
Finishing nails or strong adhesive tape, knife, sandpaper, coping saw.
To make the template. Cut the foil to a shape 10cm (4″) larger all around than the area you wish to rub, and tape it loosely against the surface in two or three places (fig.1).
☐ Work over the foil with a stiff brush, (a nail brush is ideal), 'scrubbing' it

into the crevices of the design.
☐ If the surface has detailing that is difficult to reach, use a smaller brush to press the foil into the corners.
☐ Apply more masking tape at intervals to hold the foil securely in place.
☐ When you have rubbed the foil thoroughly onto the surface, the contours and details beneath will be sharply visible through the foil.
☐ Feel carefully over the foil template with your fingers, pressing firmly to make sure the foil lies flat against the surface beneath.
☐ Remove the tape and pull the foil away very gently and carefully so that you do not damage the impression. This can be difficult to do and some people prefer to use the "board and shaving foam" method.
☐ Spray the foil with a thick coat of shaving foam and then press the board against the foam until it lies flat up against the surface.
☐ Holding the board in position with one hand, untape the foil, and fold the edges of the foil back over the board.
☐ Pull the board vertically away from the surface (fig.2).
The shaving foam has the effect of a suction cup which pulls the foil away from the stone in one piece.
To make the cast. Lay the board, foil side up, on a table, and bend back the edges from under the board to form a 'well' around the template.
☐ Place the strips of wood around the foil 'well' so that the weight of the liquid plaster will not push the walls out of shape (fig.3). Hammer the strips roughly together with nails, or bind around the frame with strong tape.
☐ Mix the plaster as described in Clay chapter 10, page 426. Pour the mixture gently into the mold. Pour in from the edges so that the plaster rises to fill the crevices of the foil template and expel any air bubbles.
☐ If you wish to hang the cast, remember to insert a twisted piece of wire for the hook before the plaster hardens. Mark the top center of the foil in the same way as was previously described for a rubber mold.
☐ When the plaster has set, turn the casting over, remove the board and carefully peel away the foil. Chip away any irregularities on the surface of the

cast with a knife, and finish off the piece with fine sandpaper if desired.
☐ The edges of the cast can be sanded smooth or, if they are very irregular, they can be sawn square with a coping saw and then sanded off.

Decorating casts
Casts made by this method can be decorated in a variety of ways.
The plaster can be left white and then polished with several coats of furniture wax to give a deep, marble-like shine.

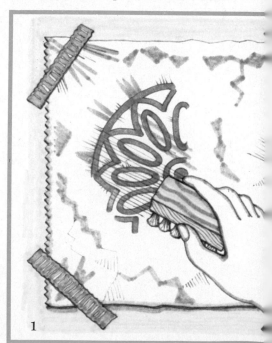

1

Peter Heinz

This polishing looks particularly attractive if the cast includes decorative interest such as cherubs or twining floral borders.

The plaster can also be painted, according to the depth of relief, with varying shades of gray poster paint for a 'stone' look, or black for an 'iron' piece, and then varnished with clear varnish if a shine is wanted.

Alternatively, and this looks particularly striking, paint the entire cast black and then color in lettering or chief features with gold, silver or metallic paint. The example shown here is a rubbing from the lid of a Tibetan box, painted in black poster paint. When the paint was dry, gold metallic paint was rubbed in very sparingly with a fingertip.

The variety of effects that you can achieve is wide—try making a series of the same cast and decorating each one in a different way. There is no need to feel limited by the neutral colors of the original piece. Experiment with

This attractive piece was cast from the lid of an antique Tibetan box. When the plaster was completely dry it was painted all over in black poster paint, and then gold metallic paint was rubbed into it sparingly with a fingertip.

bright colors for a simple 'pop' look, or soft, pastel shades on more decorative pieces.

When completed, casts can be hung on walls or left flat on tables or shelves where they look very striking.

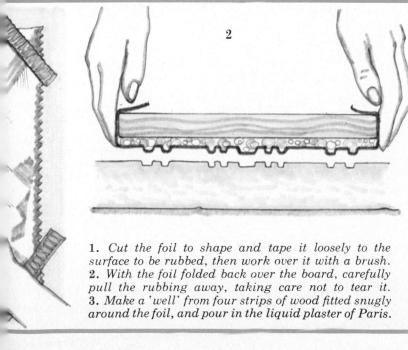

2

1. *Cut the foil to shape and tape it loosely to the surface to be rubbed, then work over it with a brush.*
2. *With the foil folded back over the board, carefully pull the rubbing away, taking care not to tear it.*
3. *Make a 'well' from four strips of wood fitted snugly around the foil, and pour in the liquid plaster of Paris.*

Joy Simpson

Candy pillow selection

What is soft sculpture? First of all it is a form of three-dimensional art. The term is applied to a wide range of objects, usually sewn from cloth and padded in some way. Sometimes it is described as 'toys for adults'—a cup of coffee or a typewriter made from foam rubber and terry cloth, or a huge pea pod made of the shiniest of satin and filled with soft batting. Some objects are definitely furniture—a padded

Steve Bicknell

reclining figure to lean on or a head-board for a bed, using quilting techniques to turn an everyday item into a piece of sculpture.

Most of all, soft sculpture is fun—so enjoy yourself. Start with some delicious candy pillows. Patterns for two sorts of chocolate and a bonbon are given in this chapter, but you can easily adapt them to make a selection of your own favorites.

Pillow forms. In the directions for the chocolate pillows the filling is placed directly inside the satin cover, which means it is not removable. If you prefer you can make a separate pillow form to go inside the satin cover, making the pieces of the form cover 1.5cm (½") larger all around than the outer cover. (See Sewing chapter 6, page 400, for suitable fabrics.)

Aerial view of rose petal chocolate, showing topstitching on the petals.

To make the rose petal chocolate pillow
You will need:
1.4m (1½yd) of 90cm (36") wide brown satin for the 'chocolate'.
45cm (½yd) of 90cm (36") wide pink satin for the rose petals.
1kg-1.35kg (2lb-3lb) synthetic filling for stuffing pillow.
45cm (½yd) of 61cm (24") 55gm (2oz) synthetic batting for rose petals.
Strong fabric adhesive.
Matching thread.
1.6m (1¾yd) of 122cm (48") wide lining fabric (optional).

☐ Make paper patterns for the pillows and the rose petals by enlarging figs. 1-4 (see Design know-how chapter 4, page 112). Seam allowances of 1.5cm (½") included on pattern.

☐ Cut out four pillow top pieces and one pillow base piece in brown satin on the straight grain.

☐ Cut out two of each petal section in pink satin, and one of each in 55gm (2oz) batting.

☐ Place two pillow top pieces with right sides facing and stitch together on one side only from A-B. Join the other two top pieces in the same way. Snip 'V'-shaped notches at 2.5cm (1") intervals along the curved edges, almost to the stitching.

☐ Place these two pieces together and stitch along the remaining two side seams. Press seams open.

Delicious candy pillows made in satin add a touch of luxury to a simple room setting. Designed by Felicity Youett.

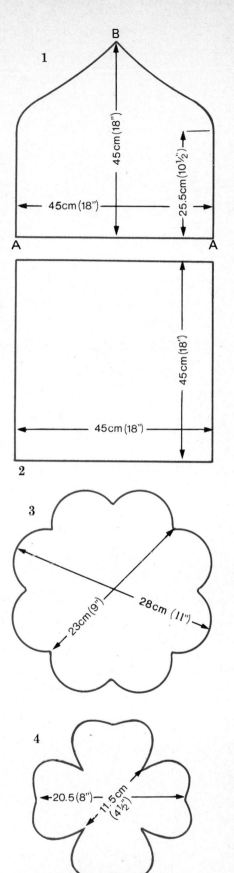

1. *Pillow top piece — cut 4.*
2. *Pillow base piece — cut 1.*
3. *Lower petal section.* 4. *Upper petal section. Cut two of each in satin and one of each in interfacing.*

☐ With right sides together pin the base piece into place, matching the corners of the base to the seams of the top. Stitch the base to the top leaving one side open to turn through. (Leave two sides open if you have made a pillow form.)

☐ Trim corners and turn pillow to right side.

☐ Insert filling until the pillow is firm (or insert the form). Then slip stitch the opening.

☐ Place the satin pieces for the larger petal section with right sides together on top of the batting section. Baste and stitch through all thicknesses, all around the edge. Trim the batting away close to the stitching and trim the seam allowance on the satin to 6mm ($\frac{1}{4}''$).

Make clips into the edge, at the angles, almost to the stitching.

☐ In the upper thickness of satin only, cut slits as shown (fig.5). Turn the petals right side out.

☐ Work lines of top stitching to make four petals (fig.6).

☐ Make up the smaller petal section in the same way and add three more lines of top stitching on each petal (fig.7).

5

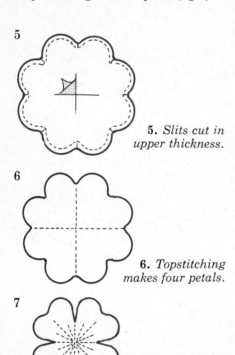

5. *Slits cut in upper thickness.*

6

6. *Topstitching makes four petals.*

7

7. *Topstitching on smaller petals.*

☐ Glue the two petal sections together at the center with the slit side of the smaller section to the unslit side of the larger one, making sure that the slits are completely covered. Overcast the two sections together at the center.

☐ Glue the larger petal section to the center of the top of the pillow, covering the slits. Turn back the petals and overcast to the pillow at several points close to the center.

512

Aerial view of almond chocolate, showing pin tucks on top of almond.

Steve Bicknell

To make the almond chocolate pillow

You will need:

90cm (1yd) of 90cm (36″) wide brown satin for the 'chocolate'.

35cm ($\frac{3}{8}$yd) of 90cm (36″) wide cream satin for the 'almond'.

About 1kg (2lb) synthetic filling for pillow and almond.

Strong fabric adhesive (optional).

Matching thread.

90cm (1yd) of 90cm (36″) wide lining fabric (optional).

☐ Make paper patterns for the pillow and almond by enlarging figs. 8-11. Seam allowances of 1.5cm ($\frac{1}{2}''$) included on pattern.

☐ Cut out two pillow side sections and two top/bottom pillow sections in brown satin.

☐ Cut one of each almond section in cream satin.

☐ With right sides together join the side strips at one short end.

☐ Work a line of stitches on stitch line on long edges and make notches 2.5cm (1″) apart almost to the stitching along both edges of side piece. This will help ease the fabric around curves when the side is joined to the top and bottom section.

☐ With right sides together, and matching point C to the seam in the side section, baste and stitch the top/bottom section to the side section and join the other side seam, so that it matches point D, as for a round pillow with a welt (See Sewing chapter 6, page 400). Attach the other top/bottom section in the same way but leave 25cm (10″), (45cm (18″) if a pillow form is used), opening to turn

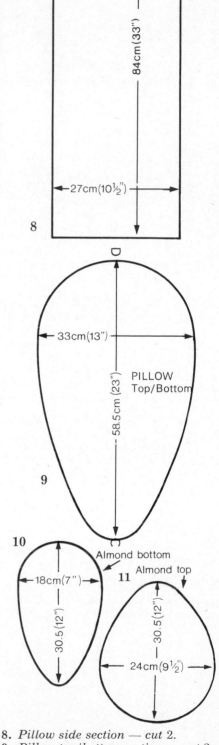

8.

PILLOW SIDE

84cm (33″)

27cm (10½″)

PILLOW Top/Bottom

33cm(13″)

58.5cm(23″)

9

Almond bottom

10

18cm(7″)

30.5(12″)

11 Almond top

24cm(9½″)

30.5(12″)

8. *Pillow side section — cut 2.*
9. *Pillow top/bottom section — cut 2.*
10. *Bottom of almond — cut 1.*
11. *Top of almond — cut 1.*

The bonbon cover laid flat to show the arrangement of stripes and circles.

through. Make 'V' notches at 2.5cm (1″) intervals all around the edge of the top and bottom sections.

☐ Turn the pillow to the right side.

☐ Insert the filling until the pillow is firm and slip stitch the opening.

☐ Stitch ten 3mm ($\frac{1}{8}$″) pin tucks across the right side of the top almond section at equal intervals, making the first and last tucks 3cm ($1\frac{1}{4}$″) from the edge.

☐ With right sides together stitch the top and bottom almond sections together, all around the edge.

☐ Cut slits in the bottom section only as for the rose petals, trim turnings to 6mm ($\frac{1}{4}$″) and turn the almond through to the right side. Stuff firmly with batting and attach to the top of the pillow in the same way as the rose petals.

To make 'bonbon' pillow

This is made from a bolster with an outer cover made in one flat piece which is then wrapped around the bolster and tied with ribbon.

You will need:

For the bolster: 1.6m ($1\frac{3}{4}$yd) cotton fabric.

1-1.15kg (2-2$\frac{1}{2}$lb) synthetic filling, or a foam bolster pad 76cm (30″) long with a 23cm (9″) diameter.

For the cover: 90cm (1yd) of 90cm (36″) wide orange satin.

1.8m (2yd) of 90cm (36″) wide green satin.

45cm ($\frac{1}{2}$yd) of 90cm (36″) wide pink satin.

70cm ($\frac{3}{4}$yd) of 90cm (36″) wide blue satin.

70cm ($\frac{3}{4}$yd) of 90cm (36″) wide yellow satin.

115cm ($1\frac{1}{4}$yd) iron-on interfacing.

2 x 90cm (1yd) lengths of 1.5cm ($\frac{1}{2}$″)

blue satin ribbon.

Matching thread.

☐ Make up a bolster 76cm (30″) long and with a diameter of 23cm (9″), as described in Sewing chapter 7, page 430.

☐ Cut out strips of orange satin, from selvage to selvage of the fabric, as follows: 1 x 63cm ($24\frac{1}{2}$″) and 2 x 9.5cm ($3\frac{1}{2}$″).

☐ Cut out strips of satin, from selvage to selvage, in the other colors as follows: 2 x 8cm (3″) wide, pink; 2 x 18cm (7″) wide, blue; 4 x 13cm (5″) wide, yellow; 4 x 9.5cm ($3\frac{1}{2}$″) wide, green and 2 x 63cm ($24\frac{1}{2}$″) wide, green (to line the striped ends).

☐ Make circular paper patterns (see Design know-how chapter 1, page 28) in a range of diameters between 7.5cm (3″) and 20cm (8″). Cut out in satin so that you have 4 blue, 4 yellow, 3 green and 3 pink circles.

☐ Position the circles, right-side-up, on the wide orange strip as shown in the photograph. Baste into place and stitch in place with a fairly small zigzag stitch.

Note: The circles can be attached with a straight stitch but it will be necessary to turn under a very small hem all around before stitching.

Taking 1.5cm ($\frac{1}{2}$″) turnings join the narrow strips on either side of the broad orange one in the order shown in the photograph.

☐ Trim turnings to 6mm ($\frac{1}{4}$″) and press onto the darker color in each case.

☐ Cut two pieces of interfacing 54.5cm x 90cm (22″x36″) and iron one piece on to each end on the wrong side of the stripes, matching one long edge of the interfacing to the raw edge of the satin

(the interfacing will reach only as far as the seam between the blue and pink stripes).

☐ Neaten one raw edge on each 63cm x 90cm ($24\frac{1}{2}$″x36″) green satin strip.

☐ With right sides together, place one green strip to one striped end, matching raw edges and selvages. Baste and stitch around the three outer edges, leaving the neatened edge of green lining free.

☐ Trim corners and turn right side out. Work a line of straight stitch through all thicknesses along the seam between the blue and pink stripes to secure the fourth edge of the facing. Work the other end in the same way.

☐ Press 1.5cm ($\frac{1}{2}$″) selvage to the wrong side on the central unfaced section of the cover. Turn in about 6mm ($\frac{1}{4}$″) and slip stitch down to neaten.

☐ Wrap the cover around the bolster and tie the ends with ribbon.

Adapt the patterns to make a chocolate selection of your own choice. Here are some real chocolates to start you off.

Coping with curved surfaces

Previous chapters on enamel have covered various techniques which involve applying enamel powder onto a dry surface. It is also possible to dust the powder onto a surface which has been coated with an adhesive. This is essential when enameling a curved surface, such as a bangle or bowl.

Adhesives

There are several water-based adhesives available, including tramil, gum tragacanth, gum arabic and cellulose wallpaper pastes which contain tragacanth.

Tramil can be bought ready to use from craft shops.

Gum tragacanth is available from craft shops ready-mixed or it can be bought in powder form from a drug store and made up at home, but this is a rather lengthy process. A disadvantage is that, once mixed, gum tragacanth tends to ferment within a fairly short time. To counteract this add a little fomaldehyde to the solution.

Gum arabic can be bought in liquid form from craft shops, and then mixed with distilled water (1 teaspoonful of gum arabic to about 0.28 lit ($\frac{1}{2}$pt) distilled water).

Cellulose wallpaper paste, which has a tragacanth base, makes an excellent substitute, is readily available and is the choice of many experienced enamelers.

Using Adhesives

An adhesive can be applied direct onto the metal blank or onto a surface already enameled (when applying a second coat of enamel).

Apply adhesive smoothly to the surface to be enameled (if you are applying it direct onto the copper this should first be prepared in the usual way). Use a sable or camel hair brush. Alternatively you might prefer to use a scrupulously clean finger tip as brushes can create air bubbles. Working over a sheet of clean paper, sift the enamel powder over the surface using a sieve. Alternatively, attach a clean piece of muslin, by means of a rubber band, over the top of an open jar and use the powder direct from the jar. If the surface to be enameled is curved, tilt the object so that the powder will adhere evenly to the whole surface.

Tip the powder which has fallen onto the paper back into the jar.

Place the object on top of the kiln for a while to dry out all the moisture before firing. If this is not done the moisture will lift the powder as it evaporates during firing.

Enameling curved surfaces

Bowls, ashtrays, napkin rings and bangles look most attractive when enameled, but their curved surfaces present a problem if you are using enamel in powder form. Enamel powder sifted onto the dry, curved surface of a bowl will fall to the bottom, leaving the metal exposed on the higher surface. Similarly, it will fall off a bangle, leaving no powder on the metal at all. This problem is easily overcome by using an adhesive.

To enamel a bangle

Note. This is not an easy technique and may take some time to master, so don't be discouraged by early results. When working on a bangle or napkin ring it is easier to counter-enamel the inside and then to enamel the outside.

You will need:

Equipment—(see Enamel chapter 1, page 106) and a stilt.

Metal blank.

Enamel powder.

Adhesive.

Emery paper.

Carborundum stone.

Anti fire-scale liquid (optional).

☐ Switch on the kiln so that it will be

Just some of the wide range of attractive items with curved surfaces available for enameling. Articles enameled by Pheobe Douglas and Betty Groocock.

Dick Miller

hot enough by the time you are ready to fire the bangle.

☐ Prepare the inside of the bangle for enameling in the usual way.

☐ Paint the outside with anti fire-scale liquid and leave it to dry.

☐ Smooth adhesive onto the inside of the bangle and dust on the powder, turning the bangle as you dust so that the whole inner surface is evenly coated. Remember to work over a sheet of clean paper.

☐ Place the bangle on top of the kiln until all the moisture has dried out.

☐ Place the bangle on the mesh stand and fire.

☐ When the bangle has cooled remove the fire-scale from the outside. It should flake off easily if anti fire-scale liquid has been used.

☐ Prepare the outside for enameling and coat with adhesive, turning the bangle as before.

☐ Place the bangle on the stand and fire.

☐ Leave it to cool completely and then clean the edges with the carborundum stone.

Other uses for adhesives

Firing two sides simultaneously. If you wish to fire both sides of an enameled article at the same time, prepare both surfaces, apply an adhesive to the underside and sift powder onto it. Place on the top of the kiln for the adhesive to dry out. Turn the object over and apply the adhesive (not essential unless the object is curved) and then sift on the chosen color. Place then object on the stilt with the underside down and fire.

Note: It is not advisable to use red enamel on the top surface and another color on the underside when working by this method as red, which is not hard-firing, tends to burn before many other colors are properly fired. (The question of colors which are hard-firing and those which are not will be dealt with in detail in a later chapter.)

Stencils and sgraffito. Another use for an adhesive is to hold powder in position when working with stencils or doing sgraffito (see Enameling chapter 4, page 496).

When working with a stencil an adhesive makes it easier to obtain a neat edge. It also prevents small specks of powder from remaining on the surrounding area after the stencil has been removed because you can lightly blow these away without disturbing the unfired enamel powder on the design. As it gives you more control of outlines you are able to produce more intricate work.

Right: dusting the inside of the tilted bangle with enamel powder, working over some clean paper.

Above: applying adhesive to a curved dish using a sable water-color brush.

Above: sifting enamel powder onto the dish, tilting it to ensure even coverage.

Above: applying adhesive to the inside of a bangle using a clean fingertip.

515

You have already discovered that to keep any shape or size of crochet motif flat, you must continuously increase either by means of extra stitches or by additional chain spaces, until you have arrived at the required circumference. This chapter now goes on to explain that by using a modified version of a crochet circle, where a number of rounds are worked without shaping, a domed shaped effect is achieved which

Add a turn-back brim to our basic hat to give it a totally different look.

forms the basis of the crown for these jaunty little hats.

Once this dome shape has been achieved, you can then continue working in rounds of crochet without any shaping at all, to form a tubular fabric which completes the hat.

This principle can be applied in many different ways, such as working the dome to the required circumference and then continuing to make a useful shopping bag—made in fine wrapping string, this would be an inexpensive and practical bag. Complete it with a braided or crocheted drawstring for a super duffel bag.

Worked to a slightly smaller size in something like raffia and finished off with two drawstrings, pulled up from opposite sides, you have a summer tote bag as an attractive accessory. Think how attractive a multi-colored striped bolster would look—you just need a little bit more know-how to complete the second domed end to match the first. This is done by decreasing the number of stitches, in the reverse sequence to which they were increased, until you arrive at the same number of stitches with which you began. Before you begin the second domed end, however, first fill the bolster with a prepared cotton or muslin shape and then complete the crochet cover. Trim each end with a thick, luxurious tassel.

To decrease one stitch

Work in ordinary single crochet, or pattern as given for the hat, until the position for the decreased stitch is reached. Insert the hook into the next

Make yourself a colorful hat in a textured version of single crochet.

stitch and draw a loop through, insert the hook into the next stitch and draw a loop through, yarn around hook and draw through all three loops on hook. When working in half double crochet, put the yarn around the hook, insert the hook into the next stitch and draw a loop through, put the yarn around the hook again, insert the hook into the next stitch and draw a loop through, yarn around hook and draw through all five loops on hook.

Draw yarn through three loops on hook to decrease in single crochet.

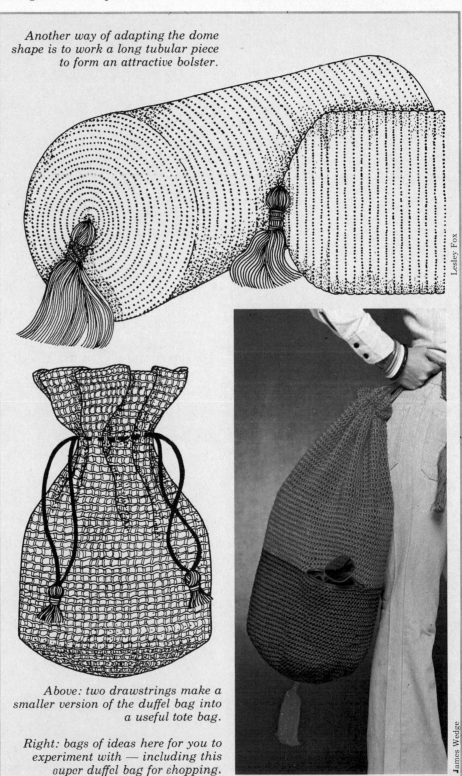

Another way of adapting the dome shape is to work a long tubular piece to form an attractive bolster.

Above: two drawstrings make a smaller version of the duffel bag into a useful tote bag.

Right: bags of ideas here for you to experiment with — including this super duffel bag for shopping.

To work this variation of single crochet, instead of working under the two loops at the top of each stitch as for ordinary single crochet, insert the hook into the back loop only of the stitch, ie, between the front and back loops at the top of the single crochet of the previous round, then into the top of the upright loop at the back and to the left of this single crochet, then complete the stitch as for an ordinary single crochet.

The basic hat

To fit an average woman's head.

You will need:

Total of 75gm (2¾oz) of any 4 ply yarn to make the basic shape, plus odd pieces for trimmings.

One No.7.00 ISR (US K) crochet hook.

Note: Yarn is used double throughout for each hat.

Make 3ch. Join with sl/st to first ch to form circle.

1st round. 1ch to count as first sc, work 5sc into circle. Join with sl/st to first ch. 6 sts.

2nd round. 1ch to count as first sc. 1sc into same place, work 2sc into each sc to end, remembering to work over the

Spiraling rounds of crochet form the crown shape of these hats — increased stitches make a curved spoke pattern.

Stitches for hats

Some of the hats shown here have been worked in ordinary half double crochet and the others have been worked in a variation of single crochet. In each case, the texture of the stitch has been heightened by carrying two separate threads of yarn loosely across the back of the work, working each stitch over these two threads.

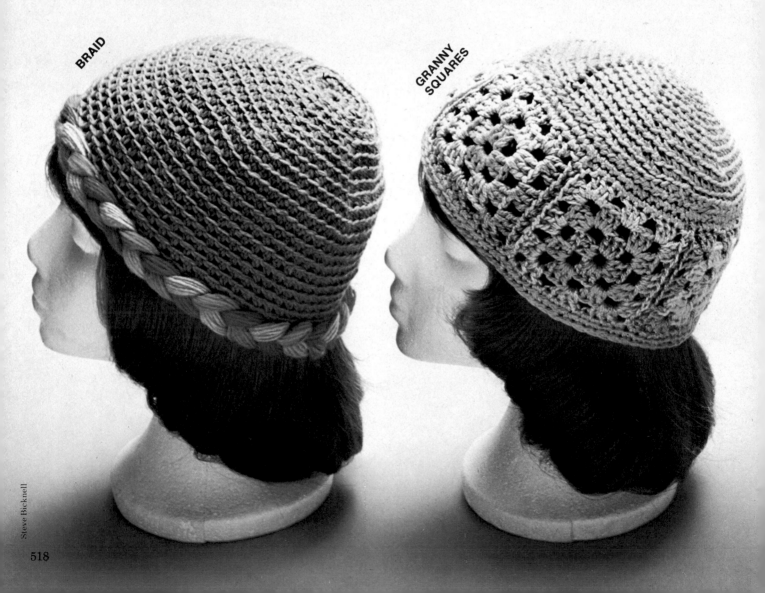

BRAID

GRANNY SQUARES

two separate threads. 12 sts. Do not join after this round, but carry on working in continuous rounds. This will be easy if you mark beg of next round with colored thread so that you do not lose your place.

3rd round. Cont in patt as given above, work (2 sts into next st, one st into next st) to end. 18 sts.

4th round. Cont in patt, work (2 sts into next st, one st into each of next 2 sts) to end. 24 sts.

Cont in patt, inc 6 sts in every round in this way until there are 66 sts.

Work 9 rounds patt without shaping. Fasten off.

Hat in random stripes (see page 516)
Work as given for basic hat in 4 colors, changing colors as desired and carrying yarns not in use loosely across back of work instead of using two separate threads and working each stitch over these strands.

Hat with turned back brim (page 517)
With double yarn and using No.5.50 ISR (US I) crochet hook, work crown as given for basic hat in half double crochet until there are 66 stitches.

Cont without shaping in rounds of half dc for a further 9cm (3½").

Change to No.5.00 ISR (US J) crochet hook and work 3 rounds of single crochet, then turn work around so that it is reversed for the brim. Change back to the original hook size and work 10 rounds of half double crochet as before. Fasten off.

Hat trimmed with braid
Using yarn double and No.5.50 ISR (US I) crochet hook, work in half double crochet as given for basic hat until there are 66 stitches.

Continue without shaping for a further 9cm (3½"). Fasten off.

Using odd pieces of 3 colors, take about 20 strands of each and make a braid long enough to fit around lower edge of hat. Sew braid in place.

Hat in granny squares
Using No.5.00 ISR (US J) crochet hook and double yarn, work crown as given for basic hat in single crochet pattern until there are 72 stitches. Fasten off.

Make 6 granny squares with 3 rounds in each as given in Crochet chapter 1, page 36, using the same crochet hook and having the yarn double throughout. Join the 6 squares into a circle.

With main color work 72 sc along one edge, then work another round in single crochet. Sew this edge in place around crown. Complete the lower edge with 2 more rounds of single crochet.

Hat in raffia
Using yarn single throughout and No.5.50 ISR (US I) crochet hook, work crown as given for basic hat in single crochet until there are 66 stitches.

Continue working in rounds of single crochet without shaping for a further 9cm (3½").

Work a round of eyelet holes to slot the ribbon through by working one double crochet into alternate single crochet with one chain between each. Complete the hat with 2 single crochet worked into each chain space. Thread ribbon through the holes if desired.

Hat trimmed with daisies
Work the basic hat.

Make one large and one small daisy as given for lampshade edging in Crochet chapter 5, page 482. Sew to side of hat.

Braids, granny squares, different sized daisy motifs and raffia are just a few ways of decorating and adapting the basic hat for a new look each time.

RAFFIA

DAISY TRIM

Resist dyeing and tritik

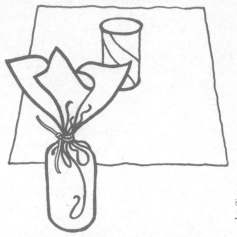

Binding fabric with cords and clips to resist dye in the dyebath (Dyeing chapter 5, page 488) is by no means the only way to produce the radiant patterns that make tie-dyeing unique. Since medieval times the search for new and intricate patterns has produced many variations, and some of the oldest techniques are among the most sophisticated. These involve tying objects into cloth to make circular patterns or 'auroras' of different sizes, or stitching and then gathering the cloth to make fascinating designs caused by the inability of the dye to seep through the gathers. This last method is known as tritik.

Tie-dyeing with objects
Many objects near at hand can be inserted into cloth 'pockets' to make effective tie-dyed designs—pebbles, corks, short lengths of match-sticks, beads, buttons, nuts and bolts and other miscellaneous bits of hardware all make useful tools for beginners to work with. The most beautiful tie-dye patterns made with objects, however, are obtained from the more demanding method of tying tiny objects such as peas, rice grains and tiny pebbles into cloth to produce delicate all-over patterns or borders. This requires a great deal of patience since the cloth must be tied around each grain or pebble separately, and the smaller the 'grain' the closer together each one should be placed.

The cord or thread used to tie objects must be dye-resistant and strong enough to allow it to be pulled very tightly. Nylon fishing line, dental floss and invisible sewing thread are all suitable.

How to bind. Start with sizable objects first. Place a tin can or glass ashtray in the center of a piece of cloth, then bunch the fabric around the object to make a 'pocket' (fig.1).

Joy Simpson

1. *To bind objects place them on the cloth one at a time, bunch the cloth up to make a pocket and tie tightly.*

Bind the thread firmly around the bunched cloth and tie the two ends together in a strong knot.
Then tie other random objects of different sizes and shapes at various dis-

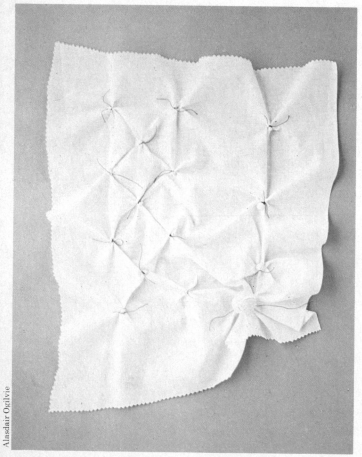

Alasdair Ogilvie

By tying objects such as peas, pebbles or buttons into cloth you can control the size and regularity of patterns.

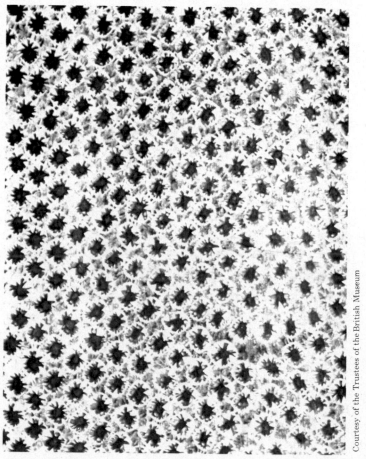

Courtesy of the Trustees of the British Museum

Tie-dyed cloth from Nigeria obtains its myriad circles from hundreds of grains tied into the cloth before dying.

tances from the central object.

It is important to realize that the purpose of the inserted objects is not to keep the dye from penetrating but to make a pucker which will affect the size and regularity of the pattern produced by the cord.

One of the oldest methods used in India actually leaves the object out. Wet cloth is placed on a bed of nails and then laboriously picked off each point and tied in minute 'ties' to make tiny circles on the cloth.

When all your objects have been tied into the cloth, wet it thoroughly and place it in the dye bath, following the manufacturer's instructions.

Design

Once you get some idea of the effect produced by sizable objects tied at random, you can plan a more careful piece of work by measuring out and marking with tailor's chalk the postion of the 'inserts'.

Different objects will, of course, make different sized circles or ovals, but by tying objects at regular intervals a repeated pattern builds up. The tinier the object the more closely they can be spaced and the more delicate will be the result.

If objects are not spherical the direction in which they are tied can also be important. Especially interesting effects can be obtained by alternating the direction of long grain rice grains, for instance.

In order to bind tiny objects tightly, it is a good idea to thread a darning or crewel needle with the thread and take a back stitch to start, leaving an end hanging. Then gather and wind the thread round the bunched cloth several times, pull it tight and tie the ends together.

When the cloth has been dyed, dried and untied, the effect will be small blurred circles or stars which give an impression of sparkling.

Sometimes, in delicately repeated patterns, the thread is carried from one 'tie' to the next without cutting so that, when dyed, a fine line connects the tiny dots of the pattern.

Colored objects are sometimes inserted into the 'ties' for the express purpose of yielding up their color on to the cloth while it is being dyed another color.

Walnut shells, for instance, will impart a brown color when simmered; blueberries, and various berries will also produce color (see Dyeing chapter 3, page 382).

Tissue paper, felt and objects that are

Muslin dress tied-dyed in bound circles with a delicately patterned ruffle made by overcasting and then gathering cloth. Tie-dyed by Anne Maile.

Steve Bicknell

Leaf pattern made by tritik (sewing). Sides of cloth were folded to middle and leaf shape sewed on. Anne Maile.

not color-fast can also be used in this manner in a simmering dye bath.

Tritik

The purpose of tritik (stitching) is the same as all tie-dyeing—to make a pattern by resisting the dye in which the cloth is put.

Tritik is done by making a row of stitches, using a running stitch, and then pulling the thread to gather the cloth as tightly as possible. In tritik it is the folds or gathers rather than the thread that prevents the dye from getting through and so makes a pattern, but your choice of thread can also affect the process.

Tritik stitches can be as small or as large as you choose, but as a general rule finer stitches should be used for more delicate motifs.

Thread must be reasonably fine to prevent holes being made in the fabric when the thread is later pulled out, but it should also be strong enough not to break when it is pulled tight. Linen carpet thread or buttonhole twist, white linen sewing thread or even doubled sewing threads can all be used because it is the folds which provide the principal resistance, not the thread.

How to stitch. Begin to sew by making a small back stitch but leave a few inches of the end hanging. This will make it easier to gather the cloth and also secure the end (fig.2).

2. Begin to sew with a backstitch. Leaving a tail makes it easier to tie.

When you have stitched the desired length of running stitch, be sure to finish on the same side of the cloth as you began. Now draw up the cloth as tight as possible and tie the ends of the thread together in a strong knot. You are now ready for the dye bath.

Always wet the cloth first and follow the manufacturer's instructions. To reduce the chances of seepage, it is safer to choose a dye which does not require immersion for a long period. Cold water dyes will dye linen, cotton, silk and rayon, and they are color fast.

As always with tie-dyeing, the cloth must be dried very thoroughly before untying to prevent any further seepage of the dye into the tied-off areas.

Design. Tritik can be used to make straight lines, squares, curves, circles, zigzags and a number of patterns from combinations of these. It is a good idea to mark in the course the thread is to take with tailor's chalk. Use a ruler for straight lines and be sure you find the straight 'grain' of the fabric. Coins, can lids or plates will produce circular patterns in several sizes.

You can make a parallel line or motifs on the cloth by folding the fabric double and stitching through both layers, or make a full motif, such as a circle, by stitching an arc using the fold line as the diameter. Later, when the cloth is unstitched and opened, the full circle will appear.

By combining different geometrical shapes, together with leaf and flower shapes, a host of other motifs can be made.

When stitching you should always start a new thread at sharp angles so that it will be easier to gather, and you

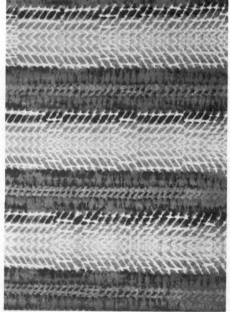

Cotton cloth has tie-dyed patterns made by overcasting. Anne Maile.

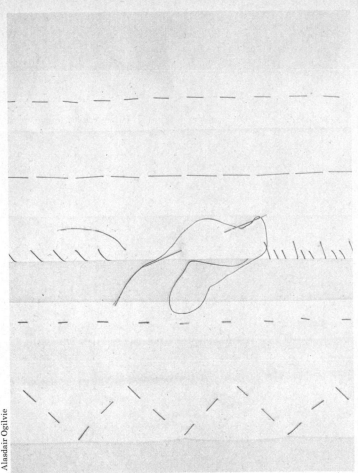

Different stitches produce a variety of effects.

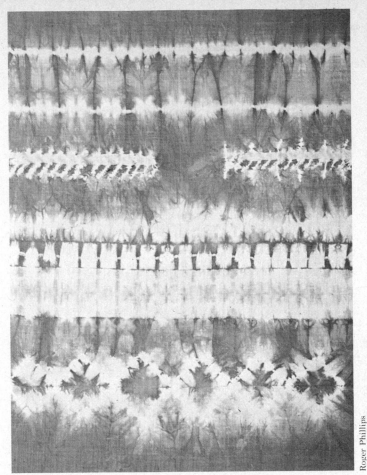

Spidery lines are the product of stitches on left.

should normally stitch the entire pattern before you begin to gather. Stitches can be criss-crossed and lines can be curved as well as straight, but in making your design, remember that the cloth must be able to be gathered.

Machine stitching, especially where long straight lines are required, can be done on a sewing machine and make the job of stitching quicker. Wind buttonhole or strong linen thread on the bobbin and use strong thread or fine linen thread for the needles. Work a long, slightly loose stitch and do not attempt to do a very long length at one time. Stop every meter (yard), knot the ends of the thread, cut and begin again. To gather, pull the stronger bobbin thread *very* gently, making sure that there is a thick knot on the other end. When pulled tight, the end you are holding can be threaded through a crewel needle and a back stitch made, or you can bind the fabric and knot to finish.

Special effects with tritik

An overcasting stitch over a fold makes a delicate 'fishbone' pattern for a border or as a central motif.

Weights can also be used to get original effects on cloth which has been gathered in circular patterns. The circle will produce a pucker when

gathered, and after being dyed in a light or medium tone an extra spot of color can be given to the tops of each pucker; this is done by hooking the center point of each pucker onto a safety pin and then attaching the pin to a heavy object such as a metal nut (fig.3). The weighted centers can then

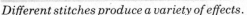

3. *Circle centers get extra color by dipping weighted ends in dye.*

be dipped in a darker dye or one of a different color. This will produce cloth with a white pattern on the background color which the material was first dyed, and there will be another tone in the center of the circles.

Wooden dowels or rectangular shapes of wood can be used to obtain particularly delicate effects on fine materials by ruching the cloth over the wood.

Be sure the wood is smooth, however, to prevent catches on the cloth.

To do this fold the fabric along the 'straight' grain of the material (or from corner to corner of a square to get a diagonal fold) and stitch a line along the fold that is 6mm ($\frac{1}{4}$") wider than the width of the dowel or wooden plank. This is to make a channel for the wood. Now insert the dowel or plank and gather the cloth as tightly as possible, using a knitting needle to ease the ruches. When the cloth is tightly packed, bind the thread two or three times around the gathered or ruched fabric and finish with a back stitch.

Dye the cloth with the ruching rod sticking up out of the bath if it is too long to be immersed.

You can also alternate round dowels and rectangular strips, but it is important to keep them at definite intervals, and parallel.

Flowers for weddings

Flowers and plants 3

Flowers have been used for centuries as personal adornment to mark special occasions and everyone is familiar with the laurel crowns of ancient Greece and the garlands that decorated the brows of festive Roman maidens. Equally familiar are the vivid leis or floral necklaces still worn by the inhabitants of Tahiti and Hawaii on days of celebration or to welcome guests.

But the best known use of festive flowers today is undoubtedly at weddings where bridesmaids' flowers, the bridal bouquet and often the floral head-dress form an integral part of the traditional ceremony.

A bouquet is really just a bunch of flowers tied together. It is the way in which it is arranged and presented that gives it a special quality.

An informal bouquet can consist of several flowers of the same kind—long-stemmed roses, for instance—tied together with a ribbon, or it can be a collection of small flowers joined into a nosegay for a child to carry. The word bouquet is derived from the French word '*bois*', meaning a wood, and probably referred originally to bunches of wild flowers gathered there.

A formal bouquet, however, is a skillful preparation, using wire to give the maximum control in creating the effect. Formal bouquets can be different shapes and sizes and consist of both natural-stemmed flowers and flowers with false stems made from covered wire, or, in the case of very formal bouquets, all the flowers can be mounted on false, wired stems.

Choosing bridal flowers

The secret of a good bouquet lies in the choice of flowers and foliage used against the dress material, its lightness, the way it balances in the hand and also its movement. Flowers at all stages of growth should be used since buds and half-opened flowers make for lightness in appearance and also help with visual balance.

Many brides want an all-white bouquet and this can sometimes cause problems because there are many whites to consider. A very white dress can make some flowers look dirty or 'off-white' when in close proximity with each other, and a very white flower—

a eucharis lily, for instance—can make a dress look positively dirty. Using green foliage to frame a bouquet will help a great deal by breaking up the hard contrast of white on white.

Some brides have a touch of color in their bouquets to link up with the color in the bouquets carried by their bridesmaids. A bouquet composed entirely of foliage can also be attractive and unusual.

Practically any flowers can be used if they can be wired and have a lasting quality of 48 hours. Their petals must be able to be sprayed with water, (sweet peas, for example, cannot be). These qualities are necessary because a bouquet is best made up the day before the wedding, covered with damp paper and then 'rested' in an airtight box in a cold place such as a fridge.

A bouquet is better if it is made up of not too many different pieces; the shape and texture of the flowers are also important.

In wedding bouquets the basic shapes are the straight or curved hand shower, the crescent spray, loose nosegay and the Victorian nosegay, where all flowers are in rings around a central rose bud.

Flowers for bouquets

White flowers which can be used include lily of the valley, hyacinth pips, white freesia, white anemones, bride gladioli, white or Christmas roses, nerine, white spray carnations (not the large-flowered single stems), eucharis lily, small arum, single spray chrysanthemums, white stock, gardenia, longiflorum lily, white delphinium, stephanotis, orange blossom, white orchids (*odontoglossom vanda phalenopsis*).

Colored flowers are easier because they provide an even wider choice and many subtle colors can be blended. Particularly beautiful colors are found in hybrid nerine, orchids, and gerbera. The single spray chrysanthemums, spray carnations, baby gladioli and freesia are all suitable flowers for bouquets.

Foliage is an important part of many bouquets and such leaves as baby begonia rex, peperomia, geranium, eucalyptus, senecio, veronica, tradescantia and the many different forms

of ivy are all useful for highlighting flowers.

Care of flowers

All flowers and foliage to be used in a formal bouquet must be fully charged with water before wiring; once they are wired they have no chance of taking up more water and rely only on overhead spraying to keep them fresh. Therefore soak all flowers up to their necks for several hours before wiring them.

No bouquet will last for very long, but the lifespan of flowers varies to some degree. For instance, lily of the valley looks sad fairly quickly, whereas orchids will hold up for two or three days.

It is sometimes possible to preserve a bouquet after the ceremony by placing it in an airtight bag containing silica gel crystals, obtainable from drug stores.

Wiring

It is wiring which distinguishes a formal bouquet, but flowers can be easily ruined by being badly wired. Special florist's wire comes in different gauges and, as a rule, the lightest wire which will hold a flower satisfactorily should be used. Over-wiring makes a bouquet look stiff and heavy; the wires should hold the flowers gracefully in position, not act as stakes.

Two types of wire are used in floral bouquets, stubb wires and silver reel wire.

Stub wires act as stalks or false stems and resemble long, thin needles. They come in several lengths and thicknesses but are normally between 18cm (7″) and 36cm (14″) long.

Silver reel wire is a fine wire used for binding flowers together or preparing them for stub wire. Silver wire comes in several gauges—the higher the gauge, the finer the wire.

All florist's wire can be purchased from floral supply houses but if you only want a small quantity try to persuade your local florist to sell you a supply.

Basic ways to wire flowers and foliage are shown in figs.1-12.

Normally flowers must be pierced through the head with silver reel wire, the wire end twisted together and then left hanging to form two 'legs' about 8cm (3″) long (fig.1). It is these 'legs' that will be used later to attach the flower to the false stem (stub wire).

Figs.2-7 show different ways to pierce the heads and petals of flowers and foliage or bind them together with reel wire.

Occasionally a heavy bud or flower is wired directly onto a stub wire or false stem by the method shown in fig.8, thus giving the flower support and doing away with step one.

Basic ways to wire flowers

Flowers for formal bouquets, nosegays and head-dresses must be wired. Fine silver wire helps support flowers and foliage, and makes wire 'legs' for mounting them onto frames or false stems.

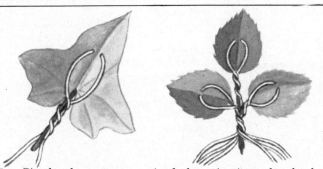

1. *Wire 'legs' for mounting flowers are made by piercing part of the flower or leaf, twisting the wire around the cut stem and leaving two 'legs' 8cm (3″) long.*

2. *Different flowers are pierced in different places; roses through lower bud.*

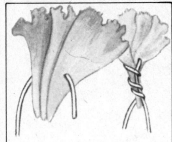

3. *Carnation petals can be wired together to make a miniature blossom.*

4. *Wire hydrangeas by twisting 3 or 4 florets into one blossom.*

5. *Narcissus and stephanotis are wired through the base, sometimes two together.*

6. *Lily of the valley, veronica and ivy trails are wired by twisting silver wire down the stem, taking care not to break the delicate side stems.*

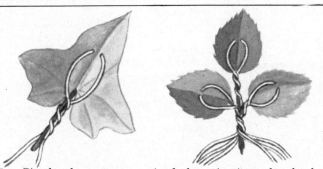

7. *Single leaves are wired by piercing the back leaf. On sprigs each leaf is wired separately and then all the wires are twisted together at the stem.*

8. *Sometimes a heavy bud or large flower is mounted directly onto a false stem or stub wire in the manner shown.*

9. *The 'legs' of silver wire secure flowers to frame as shown.*

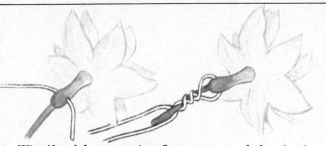

10. *Silver wire also binds 'legs' to stub wire which is covered with floral tape.*

11. *Heavy blossoms are mounted on one stub wire, then fixed to a longer one.*

12. *Parts of a spray are wired individually, then put together again.*

Barbara Firth

Unless otherwise directed, always cut away all but about 2.5cm (1″) of the natural stem. The remaining stem is used for twisting silver wire around.

Gutta percha is a special tape made from rubber and used to cover false stems. It comes in green, white and skin tone and can be bought, like florist's wire, from floral supply houses. Gutta percha does not need to be tied off since it sticks to itself. It is normally applied by spiral binding down the stem to cover it.

A pair of florist's scissors with serrated edges and a fine water spray are two other essentials in making formal bouquets.

To make the head-dress

You will need:

Silver reel wire in 0.28mm (gauge 29).

Baby ribbon, 1.5m (1½yd).

1 large head hydrangea (small flowered).

6 stems paper white narcissi.

2 large carnations.

Ivy foliage.

36cm (14″) covered milliner's wire, available from milliner's supply shop, or use two 36cm (14″) stubb wires.

Gutta percha tape and scissors.

☐ Make the circle frame by bending the milliner's wire into a circle and overlapping the ends by 1.5cm (½″), or bind two stubb wires together with silver wire, wrap gutta percha around them and bend to form a circle.

☐ Bind silver wire and then gutta percha around the overlap to hold ends together and form a complete circle to which flowers will be added one at a time.

To wire flowers. Each flower must be wired with silver reel wires cut to lengths of about 15cm (6″). You can vary the amount and types of flowers shown here or use different ones altogether, still following the diagrams showing different methods of wiring.

Paper white narcissi. Cut flowers from the main stem and pierce each blossom through its base with silver wire (fig.5), twisting the ends together and leaving two 'legs' hanging down (fig.1).

Hydrangea. Pick 2 or 3 flowers from the large round head and bind them together to make a tiny bunch (fig.4). Make several of these.

Wedding flowers are one of the most traditional and elaborate uses of flowers and they often seem mysterious concoctions. Once the basic principles of wiring flowers are understood, however, formal bouquets, Victorian nosegays and floral head-dresses can be made in the styles shown here or using other flowers recommended in the text. Designs by Olive Middleton, head teacher at the Constance Spry Flower School.

Carnation. Flowers are normally used whole but carnations are an exception because sometimes they are too large for the arrangement. Peel back the base of a flower and pull out a few petals. Place 3 or 4 on top of each other and bind with silver wire (fig.3).
Ivy. Pierce and bind each leaf (fig.7).
To mount flowers on frame, hold the frame between thumb and forefinger with the other side of the circle resting on your wrist.

☐ Place on the flowers and foliage one at a time, binding the 'legs' as one wire around the frame (fig.9). Flowers should overlap slightly to give a thick effect. Work around all but 1.5cm (½") of the frame, and tie your ribbons on to the remaining space.

Victorian nosegay
you will need:
Stubb wire, 0.56 mm (gauge 23) x 17.5 cm (7") long.
Silver reel wire, 0.31mm (gauge 28) and O.28mm (gauge 29).
Nosegay ruffle or paper doily.
Gutta percha tape and scissors.
1.37m (1½yd) ribbon.
Flowers
1 large rosebud for center.
7 rose buds.
1 hydrangea.
2 carnations.
Buds of border carnations.

Victorian nosegays are made by arranging circles of different types of flowers, usually of a different color, around one central flower (here a rose) and finishing off with a lacy frame.
To wire flowers. The rose in the center is wired by cutting off the stem to 1.5cm (½") below the sepals (the bump above the stem) and piercing through the ovary (ie the seed box) (fig.8). Use stubb wire for extra strength.

☐ 1st circle: carnation buds wired with 0.31mm (gauge 28) silver wire. Pierce through lower part of bud (fig.2).

☐ 2nd circle: rose buds are wired as above, but this time use 0.28mm (gauge 29) silver wire.

☐ 3rd circle: hydrangea, wired with 0.28mm (gauge 29) silver wire by binding 3 or 4 flowers picked from a head (fig.4).

☐ 4th circle: peel 3 or 4 carnation petals from the head of a flower and place them on top of one another. Pierce and wire together (fig.3).
To bind the bouquet together using 0.31mm (gauge 28) silver wire. Start with central rose and wrap wire around it a few times. Then begin to add other flowers in order of rows, working wire twice around each circle before adding the next one. The wire 'legs' of the flowers make up a central 'stem'.
Bind in a circular motion keeping the

silver reel wire in one place until all the flowers have been included, then take the silver wire in a spiral to the end of the 'stem'.
When the nosegay is completely bound, trim the central 'stem' to about 11.5 cm (4½"), slip on the doily and cover the remaining 'stem' by wrapping gutta percha around it. Ribbons can now be tied on the 'stem' or 'handle' to complete the bouquet.

Hand shower
You will need:
Stubb wires, about a dozen 0.71mm (gauge 21) x 36cm (14") and about a dozen 0.57mm (gauge 24) x 25cm (10"). Silver reel wire in 0.31mm, 0.28mm, 0.20mm (gauges 28, 29, 32).
White gutta percha tape.
1.5m (1½yd) nylon taffeta ribbon 2.5cm (1") wide.
Flowers
10 stems lily of the valley.
24 pips of stephanotis.
10 white roses with leaves.
5 trails of ivy.
1 pot veronica.
To wire flowers
Lily of the valley. The stem itself is wired as shown in fig.6. Use 0.20mm (gauge 32) silver wire and start at the bottom of the stem, gently twisting wire upward between the bells. Great care is needed to avoid pulling too tightly and cutting the stem.
Stephanotis is wired through the base of the flower (fig.5) using 0.28mm (gauge 29) silver wire.
Roses must have stems cut to varying lengths of between 5cm (2") and 15cm (6") and are then wired with 0.57mm (gauge 24) x 25cm (10") stub wires (fig.8) to give the flowers enough support. Cut the stub wires to the length of each natural stem.
Rose leaves should be wired in sprigs of three but each leaf in the sprig must be wired separately (fig.7). Use 0.28mm (gauge 29) silver wire.
Ivy trails are wired like lily of the valley by twisting 0.20mm (gauge 32) silver wire around the natural stem (fig.6).
Veronica is kept in natural sprays and wired with 0.31mm (gauge 28) silver wire wound around the stem like ivy trails (fig.6).
Mounting the flowers. Once you have prepared the pieces with silver wire they must be mounted on false stems of stub wire and then each stem must be bound with gutta percha before assembling the bouquet.
To mount wired lily of the valley use 0.71mm (gauge 21) x 36cm (14") stub wire according to the method shown in fig.10. Notice that the top of the stub wire is bent into a hook. Bind the wire and the sprig together with 0.20 mm (gauge 32) silver wire and then

cover the false stem with gutta percha. Mount roses on 0.71mm (gauge 21) x 36cm (14") stub wire by binding with silver wire to the previously wired natural stems (fig.11). Cover with gutta percha.
Each stephanotis has to be guttaed (ie covered with gutta percha) over existing silver wire and then re-created into sprays by binding 3 to 5 pieces on to a 0.71mm (gauge 21) stub wire (fig.12). Then gutta percha the spray.
Mount foliage on remaining stub wires (fig.10).
You should now have some 30 pieces ready for assembly.
Build the bouquet by starting at the bottom, which comes to a point, and working upward, broadening the design as you go. The flowers get bigger around the center. This can be done by standing and looking in a mirror.
☐ Using 0.29mm (gauge 28) silver wire add the pieces, one at a time, binding in a circular motion (fig.13a). As they build up, the pieces begin to form a central 'stem'. The last third of the bouquet is bent backward (fig.13b) to make the shape.

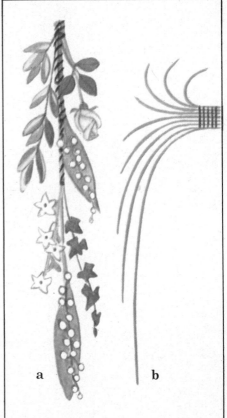

a   b

13. Diagrams show how a wedding bouquet is built up from the bottom.

When all the pieces have been bound into the bouquet, trim the 'stem' to about 11cm (4½"), cover with gutta percha and tie on ribbons to complete the bouquet.

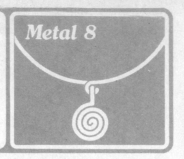

Decorative tin can cutting

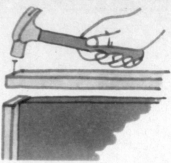

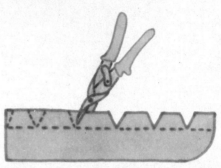

1. *Beading or strips of wood are nailed around the base for a neat finish.*

Tin cans can very easily be cut up and used to make collages. Flattened tin cans can be combined with bric-a-brac to represent anything from a vintage car to abstract designs; decorations for the seasons of the year, candle holders, surrounds for clocks and you can even make door plates.

Tools
The tools needed are simple and inexpensive.
Tin-snips available from hardware stores are used for cutting outlines.
Ordinary household pliers (combination pliers) and **round-nosed pliers** for holding and bending the tin.
A small anvil is useful but you can make do with a piece of hardwood.
Mallet for flattening the tin-cans. (A mallet is, in effect, a large wooden hammer. If you do not have a mallet you can carefully bend the tin open by hand, and then place it between two pieces of wood and use a hammer to flatten it. This method prevents the tin cans from being dented by the hammer blows.)

Materials
Apart from tin cans and an epoxy adhesive, little else is needed to finish the object, other than paint, varnish and bric-a-brac.

Collages
You can use any design you like to make a metal collage—vintage cars work especially well—and the amount of detail and authenticity depends entirely on your own effort. Find a good reference book in your local library, then make full-scale drawings to work from, lay the completed pieces on the design and then assemble onto a chosen base such as plywood.

Preparing tin cans
The tin cans must be thoroughly cleaned—gum and glue can be removed with turpentine. Remove the tops and bottoms of the cans with a can opener. Turn the cans on their sides and in the same way remove the collars or rims from top and bottom with the can opener. If your can opener cannot do this use the tin-snips to cut off the collar. Do not throw the leftovers away

as they will be useful later.

How to flatten tin cans
The tin cans must now be cut along the joins with tin-snips.
Open out into flat sheets and use the mallet to flatten the metal completely.

Vintage car collage
You will need:
Backing board with beading (or use a standard picture frame). Plywood will do for the board—it must be slightly larger than the overall design of the car.
Flattened tin cans—a variety of tins with silver and brass colors.
Epoxy adhesive.
Copper wire for the steering column, gear lever, window outlines, and so on.
Assorted odds and ends such as a tire valve screw, mirror screws and nails for making headlights, radiator caps and hub caps.
Cardboard for making templates.
Finishing nails.
Grease pencil or sharp wax crayon.
☐ Tack the beading around the backing board. Use finishing nails and join as shown (fig.1).
☐ Use the cardboard to make templates from your design. To do this cut pieces of cardboard to the size and shape of each separate piece of metal that will be required for the flat surfaces. Leave the running board, wheels and mudguards till last.
☐ Place the templates on the flattened pieces of metal and use a grease pencil or sharp wax crayon to draw the outline. Use metal with a brass finish for some parts of the design and a silvery finish to contrast, and detail the various sections. You can use gloss paint to add more detail where it is needed.
☐ Use the tin-snips to cut out the various shapes. Assemble these on the backing board and glue into position.
☐ The wheels can be made from lids, if they are the correct size; the spokes should be cut from a different colored metal.
☐ Use a nail with a large head to represent the hub cap. Nail it through both the center of the spokes and the wheel to hold them in position. Do not nail it flat but let it stick out about 6mm ($\frac{1}{4}$").

2. *The cut-out V-shapes form tags which are shaped and glued to the base.*

☐ The projecting mudguard is attached to the base by a tag. To find the length of the mudguard lay a piece of string along the line of the mudguard and mark it. Mark the length off on a piece of metal, making it 12mm ($\frac{1}{2}$") wide with a further 6mm ($\frac{1}{4}$") for the tag.
☐ Cut out the mudguard and shape with tag. Then cut small V-shaped notches along the tag (see fig.2).
☐ The tag must now be bent to an angle of 90°. To do this, place the length of the mudguard against the edge of the anvil, and hammer the tag down (fig.3).
☐ Carefully bend the mudguard to follow the curve and use glue along the tags to keep the mudguard in position.
☐ Repeat for the other mudguard. The running board is made in the same way.
☐ Using string to get the required length, cut pieces of copper wire and glue them to form the door and window outlines. Do the same for the gear-lever and the driving shaft. You can add as much detail as you like—for example, use the tire valve to represent the headlight, and so on.
☐ Paint parts of the bodywork if you want to add some color.
Work as neatly as possible and do not use too much glue or else the metal will become sticky and look untidy.
You can make countless other collages. Take designs from old magazines, and trace them and build up the collage using the same method as you did for the car.

3. *The tags are bent to 90° before the length of metal is curved.*

5. *The outside of enlarged decoration is a variation of the interior design.*

Candle holders and decorations

Candle holders and decorations look complicated to make, but if you work in stages and complete one layer at a time they are not at all difficult. A large candle holder is an ideal center piece for a table on a special occasion. You can make simpler versions of candle holders and adapt them for Christmas decorations. But if you do this, remember that the ends of the holders are sharp, so keep well out of reach of children.

Decorations, such as the star in fig.4, can be made by using lids of various sizes. The lids can be used singly or combined for more intricate effects.

☐ Use a wax pencil or crayon and draw the design on the lid (fig.4a).

☐ Draw the lines on the outside of the star, but do not cut out. The very small sections on each side of the star's tips must be completely cut out (fig.4b). Then cut parallel lines on the waste side of the star between the points as shown (fig.4b).

☐ Using pliers, twist each section so that the short outside end is at right angles to the lid. Twist each piece in the same direction (fig.4c).

☐ Using the round-nosed pliers, curl each section (fig.4d).

This completes the decoration but if you wish you can paint it. To make a larger decoration you can also combine the first design with another larger lid, cut and curled as shown (fig.5). This idea can be varied in many ways, but the basis of it is always the sections which are cut into lengths and then curled. The 'inside' shape of the pattern does not have to be a star—it can be a circle, square or irregularly-shaped star.

Above: a vintage car made from tin cans. The amount of detail is optional; wire can be used to outline door panels and windows. Designer S. Dalby.

4. *The star is used as the basic **design**:* **a.** *detail of design;* **b.** *strips cut on waste side;* **c.** *strip ends twisted;* **d.** *the twisted strips are curled.*

6   7   8   9

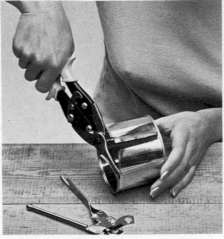

The collar and seam of the tin can is removed completely.

The smaller can for the inside of the holder is cut into narrow strips.

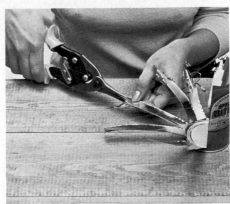

The larger can has wider strips with ends further sub-divided which are curled for a more intricate pattern.

The strips curl as they are cut but they may need to be curled more to fit in the larger can.

The strips on both cans are curled and adjusted so that the small can fits into the larger one.

Above: the candle holder in the center is made up of 4 large cans, cut and shaped in a definite pattern. Designer Stuart Dalby. The other two candle holders are less controlled in design and look intricate, but are in fact easy to make. Designer Sue Norris.

6. *After the collar around the top is removed the tin is cut into broad strips.* 7. *The strips are then cut into any number of sections.* 8. *V-shapes cut into the ends.* 9. *Ends curled.*

Candle holders are made in the same way as the decorations, but a number of tin-cans are used. These are particularly successful because they sparkle and reflect the light from the flame. Printed cans as well as plain cans can be used. Select various sizes so that they fit inside each other. The height of the candle holder depends on the height of the candle, but if the holder is fairly deep you can always increase the height of a short candle by placing another tin underneath it inside the holder.

To make a candle holder

☐ Select at least 2 tin cans which fit inside each other.

☐ Using the tin-snips, remove top collar or rim from the inside can and also the seam along the side. The seam must be taken off completely to the base of the can. Discard this piece.

☐ Cut down the sides of the can with the tin snips—the smaller the can the narrower the strips of metal should be.

☐ The strips will curl as you cut them but the curl can be tightened by winding them with pliers.

☐ Remove collar and seam from the next can and cut strips slightly wider than those for the small can.

☐ Open out the sides, like the petals of a flower, and place the small can inside it.

☐ Cut and curl the strips to make an attractive arrangement.

☐ Cut and curl the large can in the same way.

If you do not like the color of the cans you can spray them with paint.

☐ Secure the tin cans to each other with adhesive.

It is not necessary for the candle to fit exactly into the smallest can. If the candle is too narrow some of the metal strips can be pushed inward to hold it in position. If it is too wide, the strips can be flattened out and then curled up around the base of the candle.

Dick Miller

Introduction to pattern

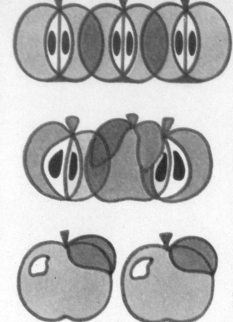

Pattern or decoration is used as a contrast to plain areas of color, and even on very plain surfaces there is usually pattern in the form of texture—a cable stitch on a sweater, the texture of a red rug or a leather bag. Other objects, such as a white porcelain bowl, which appear to have no pattern are, in fact, very finely-textured if you look closely.

Plain or pattern? Pattern is often best enjoyed in contrast with plain. How many quite ordinary rooms contain far too much pattern? This riot of decoration on tiles, pillows, curtains and wallpaper—not to mention all the things that get put on mantelpieces or hung on walls—is fighting for attention. How much better they can look with a bit of restraint: plain upholstery with richly patterned pillows, a plain dress to highlight a complicated belt or a brilliant stained glass window reflecting onto a white wall. So be selective and choose patterns with care.

What is pattern?

Pattern arises from arrangements of the basic elements: shape, line, tone, texture and color, and from mixtures of some or all in two or three dimensions. It is basically geometric, abstract or representational in shape. None of these categories is completely clear-cut and they are all interrelated.

Geometric pattern develops from shapes and lines, or parts of them, often repeated. Such patterns can easily grow from technical processes like weaving. Stripes and tartans are straightforward to weave, giving strength through evenness. Bricks are bonded in regular patterns which are functionally strong. Geometric pattern can also be painted or printed on a flat surface (see Design know-how chapters 1-10 for instructions on drawing basic geometrical shapes such as circles, squares and hexagons).

Abstract comes from the Latin 'abstrahere' meaning 'to select from'. Abstract patterns, in the strict sense of the word, are intended to convey the *essence* of the object rather than its concrete representation, or what it actually looks like. Abstract patterns can show geometrical shapes but they

can also contain random ones which arise from playful, non-structural processes like scattered color or splash painting. Such patterns may easily suggest a mood—they may echo shapes or colors which are recognizable like factory chimneys or forest trees.

Representational patterns depict 'real' objects deliberately and realistically but usually in a somewhat simplified way. 18th-century floral chintzes, for example, contain acceptable symbols for flowers. In the following chapters on representational pattern, natural and man-made objects are looked at. These could be a single leaf with its internal structure of veins, for example, leaves grouped together or the patterns which are found in buildings and streets.

Above: patterns of apples. The top three apples are arranged in a geometric design, the pattern below has an abstract quality and the bottom two apples are drawn representationally.

Below: the room contains plain areas of color and a variety of patterns.

Victoria Drew

Liz Whiting

Creative ideas 19

Tin can daffodils

Flowers cut from tin cans can be designed on real flowers or otherwise abstracted using the shape of the can to create the flower. To make these daffodils you will need 35mm film cassette cans for the flower centers, tin can lids or sheets of tin for petals, tin snips, epoxy glue, and silver spray paint or gloss paint.

Cut out petal shapes with tin snips using two lids to make the double petals. Glue them together so the petals alternate. Glue the cassettes to the centers to form the trumpet. Gently bend the petals toward the center.

The stems must be strong to support the flower head so cut a long strip of tin twice the width of the required stem, cutting out a leaf shape as you go. Fold strip in half along its length. Fold top end of stem back and glue to flower head. Either spray with silver paint, or colorful gloss paint.

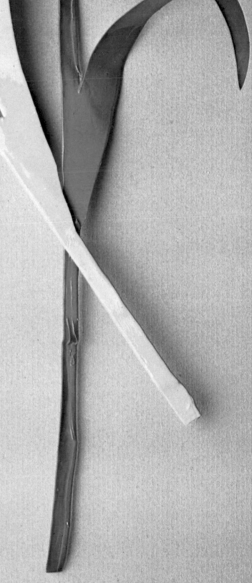

Re-cycle tin cans and film cassette cans by making these showy daffodils.

Peter Heinz

Iain Reid

How to make 'sculptured' boxes

Once the basic principles of box-making have been mastered, it's fun to make up some interesting variations. Unusual boxes like these make enchanting gift containers at birthdays, anniversaries, Easter or Christmas, or they can be used by themselves as toys or decorative objects.

Make the house on a large scale, add acetate windows and you have a doll's house. Make it on a still larger scale for a bazaar stand or a shop window display.

If boxes such as these are to be kept for any length of time, it is best to protect them with transparent plastic film, or seal them by painting with oil or emulsion paint and then varnishing them.

These boxes can be constructed of different thicknesses of cardboard, depending on the purpose for which they are intended. All of them require some scoring. See Paper chapter 12, page 422, for the type of glue and cardboard to use and how to score.

Constructing fancy boxes is a question of thinking 3-dimensionally. A box needs sides, bottom and top, and, as each of these areas has to be attached to its neighbor, flaps to tuck or stick in place.

The basic square or oblong-shaped box can be adapted to any size. Its appearance can be changed by adding shaped ends which can be stuck on at the last minute or included in the pattern, as in the duck illustrated (fig.3). Adapt fig.3 by changing the drawing of the duck into a tiger, a cat, or whatever you wish. You can also cut out pictures of animals from books and magazines and build these up into a 3-dimensional form.

To make the boxes
You will need:
Steel ruler.
Cardboard.
Paper adhesive.
Knife or sharp cutting tool.
Narrow and double-sided transparent adhesive tape.
Poster paints.
Felt-tipped pens, or decorative papers, pictures of animals such as a duck, tiger or cat.

A handsomely decorated chest filled with goodies is a real treasure trove.

Treasure chest. For the base of this box, use either a ready-made shallow, oblong box base or make one as shown in Paper chapter 13, page 478.

☐ Cover the whole box with wood grain paper.

☐ On a piece of cardboard draw a circle, the diameter of which equals the width of the top of the box base.

☐ Draw another circle about 1.5cm (½") bigger, outside the first circle.

☐ Score along the smaller inner circle. Cut out around the larger circle and cut tabs into it.

☐ Remove alternate tabs (fig.1). Cut the tabbed circle in half. Turn in tabs. These two halves of a circle represent the domed ends of the treasure chest lid:

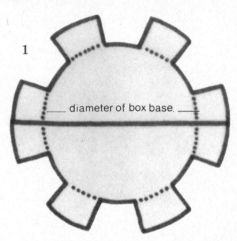

diameter of box base

1. *Circle is scored, tabbed and halved.*

☐ Cut a piece of cardboard the same length as the box base but wide enough to form a dome over the two semi-circular ends, plus a 6mm (¼") tab to stick to the back of the box (fig.2). Score along sticking tab edge.

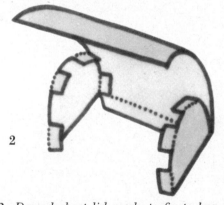

2. *Domed chest lid ready to fix to box.*

☐ Stick dome over the semi-circular end tabs. Cover completed domed lid with wood grain paper.

☐ Stick dome to top back of box base at the sticking tab. Trim treasure chest with gold paper. Fill with chocolate coins for a child's gift, or put a necklace in for an adult.

Roger Phillips

Victoria Drew

This cheerful looking little duck box would make a delightful toy for a child.

Duck. This little duck-shaped box has a base measuring 5cm sq (2"sq).

☐ Draw to scale on yellow cardboard the plan in fig.3, with the duck shape on opposite sides of the square base.

☐ Cut out on solid lines. On the right sides score along orange dotted lines and on wrong side along black.

☐ Paint eyes with white poster paint and add other details with felt-tipped pens.

☐ Fold as in fig.4, glue the tabs and stick the box into shape.

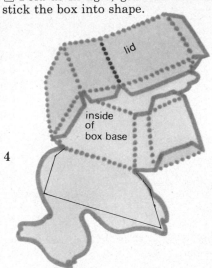

4

4. *Fold the box into shape for gluing.*

3. *Plan for duck-shaped box with dotted lines showing scoring, and tracing pattern of duck outline to actual size.*

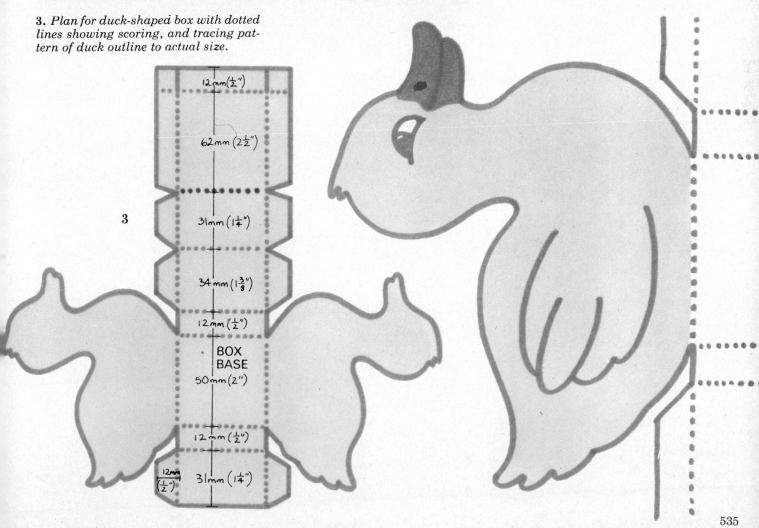

12mm (½")

62mm (2½")

31mm (1¼")

34mm (1⅜")

12mm (½")

BOX BASE

50mm (2")

12mm (½")

12mm (½") 31mm (1¼")

3

You can also create your own shapes by working out the necessary relationship between the sides and the lid on a piece of squared paper before actually cutting it out of cardboard.

Start by thinking of something as simple as a house. It starts off like an oblong box, but the 'flapped lid' is extended to follow the gable line.

Cottage. With clever tucking and cutting, this cottage will hold together quite well when only one flap is stuck and can thus be stored flat.

You could make a whole village of these boxes to amuse children. Vary the decorations and sizes of the buildings.

☐ Copy the plan (fig.5). Cut along solid lines, score and bend along dotted lines.

☐ Cover the roof area with decorative paper. Fold the plan into a house shape tucking base flaps into holes. Add door and windows from colored magazines or with felt pen or paint.

☐ Gum the final flap or stick it in place with transparent adhesive tape.

5. *Cut-out plan for the oblong cottage-shaped box photographed below. Clever tucking and use of flap tabs means the cottage requires gluing in one place only (the tab on the far left on the plan), and it can be folded flat for storage as shown in the small diagram.*

3-dimensional cat. Now look at the same idea applied to something as apparently complicated as a 3-dimensional cat. It starts with a rectangular base like an ordinary box. But the two sides are shaped like a cat and the rest of the box follows all the contours of the cat's back and head.

☐ Draw the simplified cat outline to any size you wish.

☐ Now measure the outline of the cat (fig.6). Use a piece of string to measure the curved line A-B, and draw line A-B² so that it is the same length. Then add on 6mm (¼") to allow for a folding tab. Measure the line B-C in the same way, and draw line B³-C to the identical length. There is no need to add a folding tab this time.

☐ Decide on the depth you wish the box to be, and repeat the image.

☐ Cut out the whole shape, allowing plenty of tabs where the cardboard will be curved (fig.7). Then score, decorate and assemble the box.

☐ Follow the same method for unusually-shaped boxes of your own design, remembering that simple outlines are most effective.

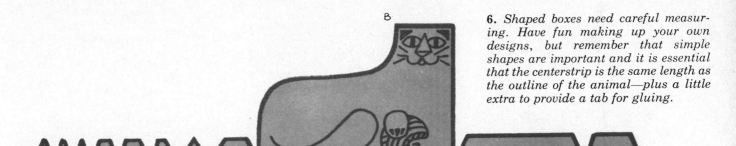

6. *Shaped boxes need careful measuring. Have fun making up your own designs, but remember that simple shapes are important and it is essential that the centerstrip is the same length as the outline of the animal—plus a little extra to provide a tab for gluing.*

This lion box, designed by Cliff Richard of Polypops, uses the same fold and flap techniques as the cottage box.

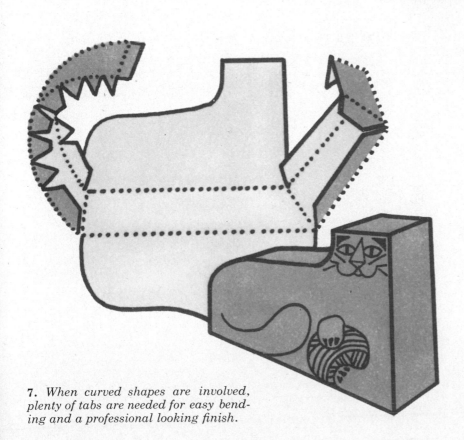

7. *When curved shapes are involved, plenty of tabs are needed for easy bending and a professional looking finish.*

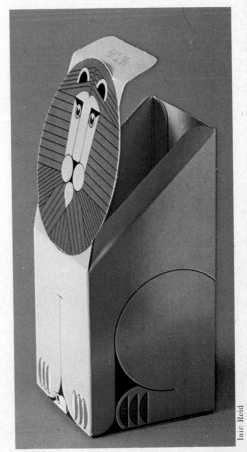

All sorts of simple molds

To shape clay on a mold

You will need:

The usual tools for rolling out a clay slab (rolling pin, canvas, sticks for controlling thickness, sharp knife, cutting wire).

Bowl or dish to act as mold.

Lining material such as newspaper. Flat shaped rasp (this is a form of wood modeling tool, rather like an ordinary file).

Lining the mold. When you have chosen your mold, prepare it for use.

☐ Non-absorbent materials such as metal or pottery must be lined, or the clay will stick to the surface instead of leaving the mold easily. Newspaper, fine linen or canvas are all suitable lining materials. Porous materials such as plaster do not need to be lined. The lining need not fit the mold exactly, but it should lie flat because any wrinkles will mark the underside of the pot.

☐ Roll out the clay as described in Clay chapter 3, page 90. Make sure that it is of even thickness, and that the surface is smooth. For small molds the clay should be about 3mm ($\frac{1}{8}$") thick.

☐ If you are molding over the shape, place the mold on the clay and draw lightly around the perimeter. Cut out the shape with a sharp knife (fig.3).

☐ Lift the clay up, supporting it on all sides, and place it over the mold (fig.4).

☐ Ease it into position slowly and gently, using the finger tips to 'form'

Molding from rolled-out slabs of clay is an easy way to make simple, shallow dishes. The clay is cut to shape, pressed over or into a suitable mold and then trimmed to fit exactly, rather like a pastry case.

The technique is very straightforward. It was used to make some very early pots and dishes, and variations of it are still used by primitive peoples. English peasant potters of the 17th and 18th century made pottery in this way and, traditionally, they decorated their work with slip. (Slip is colored clay, wetted down so that it forms a creamy liquid. Its decorative applications are covered in a future chapter.)

Choosing a mold

Any one of a variety of household objects can be used as a mold, depending on the shape you desire.

Most simply, clay can be molded over or into saucers and dishes. Choose a fairly shallow shape over which the clay can be 'fitted' without folding.

Remember that clay laid inside the mold will make a dish smaller than the original shape, and clay formed over the mold will give a larger dish (figs.1 and 2).

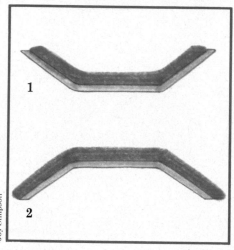

Joy Simpson

1,2. *Clay laid inside mold makes a smaller dish, outside a larger dish.*

Dick Miller

A group of molded bowls, left: designed by Siddig El' Nigoumi; back: Colin Pearson; right: Elizabeth Duncombe.

the edges around the sides of the mold (fig.5).

☐ If you are molding into a dish, cut out a rough shape in clay, place it over the mold and ease it down gently, working from the sides—do not press into the clay, but gently feel to see that it fits into the mold (fig.6). It must be supported completely by the mold before any further work can be done.

☐ Trim away the surplus clay from the edge of the dish with a cutting wire. Hold the wire taut as you work, and press it down through the clay onto the edge of the mold (fig.7). Then, using the edge as a guide, pull the wire across the clay to remove the surplus (fig.8).

☐ If you are molding inside a shape, allow the clay to dry until it shrinks away from the edges of the mold. This process will take an hour or so, after which it can easily be removed from the mold.

☐ Smooth away any roughness around the rim of the pot with a rasp.

☐ If you are molding over a shape, carefully remove the clay before it dries because when it starts to shrink it will contract onto the mold and crack.

Experimenting

There is no need to feel limited by the shapes provided by saucers and bowls, or even by the rather similar shape of the 'frisbee' used in these illustrations. Try the pan of your kitchen scales, which will give a large, attractive fruit-bowl shape, or an unusual 'scoop' for candy or nuts, depending on the design.

A roll of paper towels, for example, laid horizontally, provides the mold for a trough, useful for seedlings or spools of thread (fig.9)

4. Lift the clay up and position it carefully over the lined mold shape

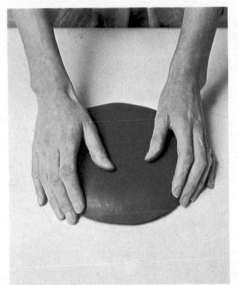

5. Ease clay gently into position, forming it around mold with fingertips.

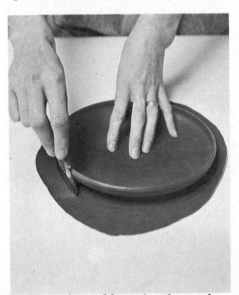

3. Place the mold on the clay and cut around the edge with a sharp knife.

7. Press taut cutting wire down through clay onto edge of mold shape.

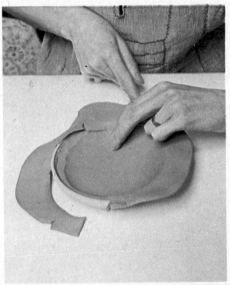

8. Using edge of mold as guide, pull wire around to remove surplus clay.

6. Ease clay down inside mold, feeling to see that it fits all around.

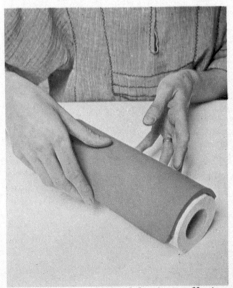

9. A kitchen roll laid horizontally is a simple and useful shape to mold on.

Nelson Hargreaves

Cloth molds. For a really large dish, a square or rectangle of cloth can be suspended from the corners of an upturned stool, or the corners of a box (fig.10). The depth of the dish so formed will depend on how tautly the cloth is suspended.

Sand bags. Alternatively, if you cannot find the exact shape you want, use a coarse linen or canvas bag loosely filled with sand. The sand can be shaken and pressed to give a hollow of the desired depth and dimensions.

If you are using an awkwardly shaped mold such as a triangle, or molding over a bag of sand or a scale pan, you will need to cut a more accurate shape out of the clay before molding it.

Make a paper pattern of the shape you intended to use (fig.11) and cut this pattern into the rolled-out clay.

This shape can be placed straight on to the mold without further trimming (fig. 12).

Plaster of Paris

If you cannot improvise a satisfactory mold shape in any other way, it is possible to make one from plaster of Paris. See Clay chapter 10, page 426. Begin by making a model of the shape you want in solid clay. Keep it simple, without sharp corners or undercutting. It should also be fairly small, particularly for a first experiment—no more than 10cm (4″) deep and 30cm (12″) long (fig.13).

Lay the completed clay model in a 'well' exactly the same as the one used for the plaster of Paris casting technique already described (fig.14).

Mix plaster and pour it over clay to cover it by about 2.5cm (1″) (fig.15).

Leave the plaster to harden, then remove the well and ease the clay out of the plaster mold. Leave to harden overnight before use (figs.16, 17).

Alternatively, ready-made plaster molds can be bought.

Using the technique

Once the basically simple molding technique has been mastered, it is a reliable way to produce shapely, attractive pots and dishes of all shapes and sizes. It also becomes an ideal way of mass-producing, on a small scale, pots for experimental purposes, such as when trying out firing, glazing or various decorations.

A forthcoming chapter deals with a variety of slip trailing techniques, all of which are worked out on a series of small, round molded dishes. If an experiment is not a success, a replica of the pot can easily be made for further practice.

12. *Place the shaped clay over the canvas bag mold, pressing it into the desired shape with the fingertips.*

Joy Simpson

10. *A cloth mold is a useful way to make a really large molded dish. Tie the cloth or canvas to the corner of an upturned stool or box, adjusting it so that the hollow is the right depth.*

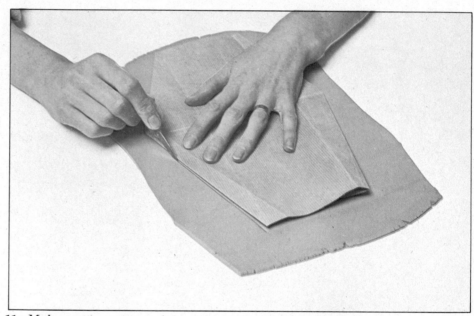

11. *Make a paper pattern of the shape and cut out of the clay.*

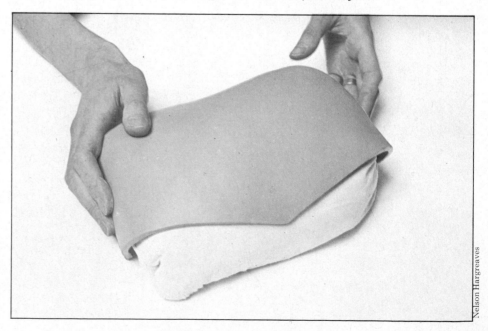

Nelson Hargreaves

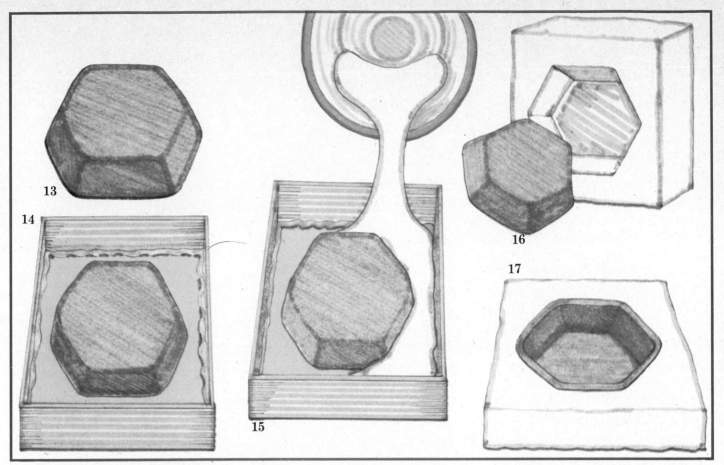

13. *Make a model of the shape that you desire in clay, remembering to keep it simple without any sharp corners.*
14. *Place clay model in a cardboard well the same as that used earlier for plaster of Paris casting technique.*

15. *Mix plaster of Paris in exactly the same way and pour it into the well to cover the mold shape completely.*
16. *When the plaster has dried out thoroughly, remove the well and ease the clay out of the finished mold.*

17. *The clay can then be rolled out, pressed into mold and trimmed to finished shape as described above.*
Below: Ready-made plaster molds can be bought in a variety of shapes from potters' suppliers.

Friendly felt ponies

Sew a felt pony. It is quick and easy to make. Designer: Ruth Beard.

542

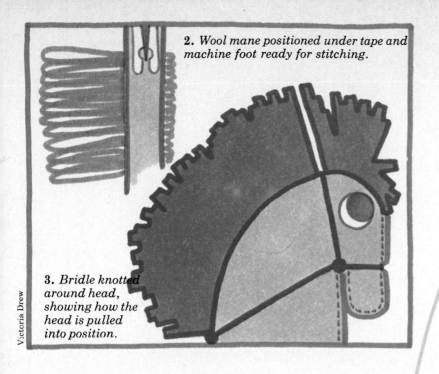

2. *Wool mane positioned under tape and machine foot ready for stitching.*

3. *Bridle knotted around head, showing how the head is pulled into position.*

Victoria Drew

Trevor Lawrence

1. *Tracing pattern for body of pony. When making your pattern, trace head in position on neck, matching lines A-B. Note that the head is pulled into position when the bridle is knotted.*

B

B

A

A

B

The first toys chapter describes how to make a simple bean bag mouse which is then loosely filled with a hard filling—split peas. This chapter shows you how to make up an equally simple shape—a pony in felt and then fill it firmly with a soft, squashy stuffing.

Felt is easy to sew and as it does not fray the pony is topstitched together on the outside with a very small seam allowance. The mane, tail and foot fringes are made from thick yarn which is an effective, quick way of getting a satisfactory effect by using a readily available material. The basic shape is so simple that you can vary it in many ways to create cart horses, circus ponies—even Zebras.

To make a pony
You will need:
Two 30cm (12″) squares of felt.
Scrap of felt in a contrasting color for the saddle.
Scraps of black and white felt for eyes.
About 30cm (12″) rick-rack braid.
About 45cm (½yd) cord for the bridle.
Ball of thick wool for mane, tail and foot fringes.
70cm (¾yd) of 1.5cm (½″) tape.
Small quantity of soft stuffing (Acrylic or other synthetic filling).
Fabric Adhesive.
☐ Trace the pattern for the body following fig.1, tracing head in position on neck (match lines A-B).
Cut out twice in felt.
☐ Measure the curved edge of the

neck and cut a piece of tape to this measurement.
☐ Unwind a small quantity of wool from the ball and wind it around three fingers several times and cut off wool.
☐ Remove the wool from fingers and place it under the foot of the sewing machine with the tape on top and to one side (fig.2), then stitch. Continue in this way until wool is attached to the whole length of the tape.
☐ Cut the loops on the side away from the tape to form a fringe.
☐ Make tail in the same way but use a 2.5cm (1″) length of tape.
☐ Place the two body pieces together with the tail between them so that the tape is covered. Leaving curved neck edge open, baste and stitch the pieces together, 3mm (⅛″) from the edge.
☐ Stuff the pony fairly firmly, pushing it down into the legs with a knitting needle.
☐ Arrange the mane in the open neck edge so that the tape is covered. Using a zipper foot, baste and stitch through all thicknesses.
☐ For the eyes cut two 2cm (¾″) diameter circles from white felt and two 1.3cm (½″) diameter circles from black felt. Glue these onto face for eyes and then glue a small amount of mane onto face in front of eyes as in the photograph.
☐ Cut two pieces of cord for bridle and arrange as shown (fig.3). Cut off any excess and put a dab of glue on each knot.

☐ From contrasting felt, cut a piece of felt for the saddle 11.5cm x 4.5cm (4½″x1¾″), rounding the corners. Stitch rick-rack braid around the edge, overlapping the braid by about 1.5cm (½″) at the join.
☐ Glue saddle in position.
☐ Make up foot fringes on 7.5cm (3″) lengths of tape as for the mane, but winding wool around two fingers instead of three.
☐ Glue foot fringes around bottom of the legs.

Variations on a theme
Zebra. By making up the pattern in a boldly striped cotton fabric and by cutting the mane much shorter and omitting the foot fringes, the pony becomes a Zebra.
Note: It will be necessary to add on seam allowances of 6mm (¼″) all around the pattern when cutting out, and also to stitch the body together with wrong sides facing and then turn it through to right side.
Circus pony. Give your pony a long flowing mane and a decorative saddle and harness (perhaps with bells) and omit the foot fringes and you will have a circus star.
Cart horse. To make a noble cart horse braid the pony's mane and tail, and give it longer and even more luxuriant foot fringes.

Painting designs on canvas

Creating your own exclusive needlepoint patterns as well as being able to match up existing furnishings are two of the many advantages of painting the design on canvas. A painted canvas is quick to work from as there is no need to keep referring to a graph pattern.

If your yarn does not cover the canvas perfectly—as sometimes happens when using cross stitch—the plain canvas will not show through because the background has been painted and will blend happily with the color of the yarn.

Ready-painted canvases are expensive and the colors and pattern often not quite what you want. So why settle for something that's not quite right. By painting your own you not only save money but at the same time create something truly original.

Choosing the design

Initially it is best to select a design that has fairly large and simple blocks or areas of color. You can attempt more detailed designs as you become more experienced and gain confidence.

For inspiration try looking through plant and flower books and adapt those designs to a more stylized form. Don't, at this stage, try to copy them exactly, though.

Another good idea is to study some of the flowing lines or geometric borders typical of the Art Deco period—on jewelry, posters and vases. Visit art exhibitions and ask at your local library for books on design know-how—you'll be surprised at how much you can benefit.

Preparing the design

Once you have chosen your design and decided what size you want, allowing room for a border if necessary, plot out the pattern on a rough piece of paper. It is a good idea now to experiment with different color tones until you have built up your design to achieve the desired combination of muted or bright shades.

As soon as you feel satisfied, you can outline the main pattern to scale onto a special piece of oil-painting paper using a black felt-tip pen. Then paint in the areas where you intend to have patches of shade, changes in tone etc.

When painting in the design it is important to choose colors which match the embroidery yarns as closely as possible.

If there are two tones of the same color which are not easy to distinguish, make one of them stronger so that the dividing line can easily be seen when you are working on the canvas.

Paint the colors of the design carefully, making a clear edge where the colors meet; do not let them merge.

Although the paint should be applied thickly enough to give a good, strong color, keep the surface as smooth as possible so that the paper will lie flat. Allow the paint to dry completely and then cover the work with a piece of plastic sheeting (available from good art supply shops and often referred to as acetate).

Borders. If you want to draw a border around the design, check that the warp and weft of the canvas are true. Use a protractor and ruler or a set square to draw the border accurately.

Alternatively, draw the border on graph paper and trace it onto the canvas, remembering to draw in the lines with indelible ink. (Do not use a dark color ink, though, if the border is pale).

Decide on the width of the border and count the number of squares on the canvas that make up the width. Draw in the other sides of the border, counting the number of squares every now and then to check that the lines are still parallel. Also take care to position the border at a satisfactory distance between the design and the edges of the work.

Painting the canvas

Suitable paints. Either oil, acrylic or water color may be used to paint the canvas.

Oil and acrylic are the most popular because they give a more durable finish. Acrylic is particularly good as it dries so quickly, too.

Select a suitable size paintbrush for the area of color to be filled in. It's worth pointing out, too, that you will find it easier to see your design if you work on white rather than buff-colored canvas.

Transferring the design. Place the painted design, still covered with the sheet of acetate, on a flat surface or board and place the canvas over it. With adhesive tape or thumb tacks, secure the canvas in position. The colors of the design will be clearly visible through the gaps in the canvas. The idea now is to transfer the design onto the canvas itself. Paint boldly on to the weave of the canvas, trying to avoid clogging up the gaps with paint. If, however, some do get clogged, pierce through the gaps with a needle before you start to embroider or the yarn may become frayed—even cut—on the sharp edges of the paint.

If you are adding a border, paint this in last so that you don't have to keep leaning across wet paint. When you have finished, carefully remove the canvas from the working surface and set it aside to dry out. Wipe down the sheet of acetate to remove any paint and store the painted design in a safe place for possible future use.

Freehand and geometric designs

There are two ways in which designs may be applied to the canvas. The one described previously is the most reliable and enables you to duplicate a pattern.

The other way is to draw direct onto the canvas. However, if you do feel inspired to attempt a freehand design, do bear in mind that canvas is expensive and mistakes can only be rectified by covering them over with a natural color. Too many mistakes will lead to a build up of paint that will reduce the flexibility of the canvas, the holes will block up completely and the canvas will become useless.

Simple geometric designs can be counted out, square by square, the outlines painted directly onto the canvas and the areas of color filled in afterward.

Peter Heinz

Above: areas showing changes of tone should show clearly through canvas. Right: painting canvas over a tracing. It is advisable to secure to a board with thumb tacks to prevent slipping.

Dark area of petals

Dark area
of leaves

Trevor Lawrence

1

2

Painting the design

1. Trace poppy design on paper with thick felt-tipped pen, marking in the tones of the two colors used.

2. There are two tones for the foliage and two tones for the flowers. Choose the color of the tapestry wool for the poppies first—you can match them to the scheme of your room—and fill in the poppies on the tracing in paints of similar shades. Then choose greens that go well with the poppies. Right. A few color scheme suggestions.

This poppy design is a fine example of the brilliant effect that can be obtained with yarn on canvas.

Poppy pillow

The flower may be worked in either half cross stitch, or tent stitch for harder wear. The appearance on the right side of the work is the same for both, but tent stitch is more thickly padded on the reverse side.

The shape of the flowers is created by using two tones of the same color. You can choose two blues for a Hima-

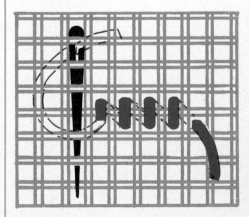

Poppies look good in shades of blue.

layan poppy, two reds for field poppies and two oranges or yellows for the Icelandic poppy.

You will need:
Double canvas, 10 threads per 2.5cm (1″), 35cm x 35cm (14″x14″).
Fabric for back and sides of pillow 27cm x 27cm (11″x11″), plus 2 strips each 55cm (22″) long and 5cm (2″) wide.
Piping cord 220cm (88″) long, covered with bias strips made from the same material used for back of pillow.
Tapestry yarn, 7 skeins off white, 4 skeins scarlet red (light tone), 3 skeins scarlet red (darker tone), 2 skeins light grass green, 2 skeins darker grass green, 2 skeins black.
Tapestry needle no. 18.
Matching sewing thread and needle.
Pillow form 29cm (11½″) sq.
To work the poppy. Mark the center of the canvas horizontally and vertically. Paint the canvas following the method given. Work the pattern in half cross stitch, starting with the poppies and leaves. When all the pattern is done, fill in the background.
To make up. Trim the canvas to within 1.5cm (½″) of the worked area.
☐ Baste the piping to the front of the canvas work.
☐ Join the gusset strip and pin to the canvas work, right sides together. Stitch through all the layers.
☐ Pipe and stitch backing to gusset, right sides together, leaving one side open. (See Sewing 7, page 430.)

☐ Turn to the right side.
☐ Insert pillow form and slip stitch along the remaining unstitched side.

Half cross stitch

This stitch is ideal for pictures. Worked on a fine canvas it can simulate gradations of light and shade.

In many stitches both sides of the canvas are incorporated into the pattern thus giving the canvas double strength. However, with the half cross stitch, as you can see from fig. B, there is only a series of vertical lines on the reverse side which don't give much additional durability, so use it for items that do not get much hard wear, such as fire screens, pillows or bell pulls.

To work the stitch. Working from left to right, bring the needle through the lower left hole of the row you wish to work and insert the needle one thread up and one thread to the right. Bring it out in the same movement one

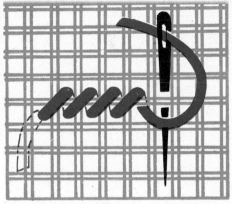

A. *Half cross stitch from right side.*

thread down (fig. A). Continue in this way to the end of the row.
Work the second row from right to left, bringing the needle out at the upper right hole of the row, either above or below the one you have just worked. Insert the needle one thread down and one thread to the left and bring it out one thread up. Continue in this way to the end of the row.

B. *Half cross stitch from wrong side.*

How to use a coping saw

It should be possible to limit the number of carpentry tools one accumulates to a few basic ones. But somehow there are always exceptions to the rule; when one saw will not do the job of another one, for example.

Although you should try to limit yourself to the necessary tools, there is always the temptation to build up a collection of specialist's tools.

For most carpentry jobs a good panel saw is perfectly adequate. But there are times when another type of special-purpose saw is essential. It can be expensive for those who want a complete workshop. But the coping saw (or jig-saw) is a special saw worth buying. A coping saw allows you to cut intricate shapes and curves in thin pieces of wood, ie not thicker than 12mm ($\frac{1}{2}$"). You can make practical, money-saving things like lamps, handbag handles or belt-buckles as well as fun things like jig-saw puzzles, mobiles or Christmas decorations. There are so many small exciting things to make with a coping saw, using wood and plywood that would normally go to waste. And you get so much reward for so little effort and expense that you will begin to wonder why you ever bought things from shops before.

Tool Box

Coping saws and fret saws

Coping saws and fret saws are used to cut irregular shapes and to cut holes in wood. They have replaceable blades about 15cm (6") long and both saws function similarly.

The difference between the fret saw and coping saw is the distance between the blade and the bow. The coping saw blade is much closer to the bow which means that you can only cut a distance in from the edge of the piece of wood.

The coping saw is all you will need for most jobs.

The fret saw is a special purpose tool: it has a deeper bow which allows you to work further in from the edge.

Putting a new blade into either type of saw is easy. Simply fit the blade into the slotted pin at the top of the saw and then into the slotted pin near the handle. Tighten the blade by turning the handle. Change direction of the blade by turning these pins and be careful not to twist the blade.

Cut on the downward stroke and hold the saw vertically. Use long strokes to avoid overheating the blade.

Using a coping saw

The inexpensive coping saw is easy to use. Perhaps the most important part of using it is to have a sturdy base to work on. Use a C-clamp with a piece of supporting wood cut with a V as shown (fig.1). The C-clamp is also a useful aid when you want to glue things together.

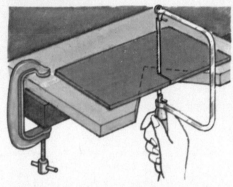

1. Position for using the coping saw.

Make sure that the base on which you work is secure and hold the piece firmly as you saw. The blade may get hot after a while—allow it to cool by putting it aside for a few minutes. The blades break quite easily so it is a good idea to buy two or three at a time.

Practice with belt buckles. There is nothing at all difficult about using the coping saw. And to get a little practice before starting on the bag handles use some scraps of plywood and cut out the belt buckle shown in fig.2.

2. Belt buckles can be made to any size or shape but the piece between the two cut-outs must not be too narrow.

You can vary the shape and size to suit your own belts but first make a drawing on a piece of paper adapting the desired measurements to fit the width of your own belt. Then cut it out with scissors before tracing the outline onto the piece of plywood.

To cut the inside holes see the step-by-step instructions on pps 550-1. It does not take long to make a buckle, and remember that it is practice so you are allowed to make mistakes to learn from them. Use 6mm ($\frac{1}{4}$") plywood for buckles and do not make the center piece less than 6mm ($\frac{1}{4}$") wide.

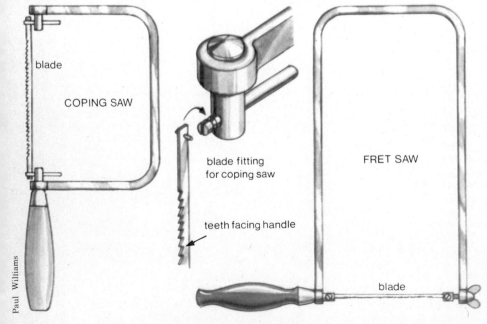

blade

COPING SAW

blade fitting for coping saw

teeth facing handle

FRET SAW

blade

Steve Bicknell

Various designs for handles. Fabric is attached to the rectangular handle by folding the fabric through the slot to the inside of the bag and stitching it. Designed by Roger Polley.

To make handbag handles

The handbag handles are cut from remnants of 3mm ($\frac{1}{8}$") plywood. They can be finished in any number of ways to match the material you use for the bag.

You can use a plywood with a mahogany (or similar) facing with clear polyurethane varnish to protect it. If there are no mahogany ply pieces available any other thin plywood pieces will do.

Since most lumber dealers and craft shops sell small remnants of plywood, the cost of the popular handbags illustrated above will be minimal yet the finished bags in shops can be very expensive.

You will need:
Tools
Coping saw and C-Clamp.
Hand-drill with 3mm ($\frac{1}{8}$") drill bits.
Ruler, pencil.
Sandpaper—fine and medium.
Materials
For two handles each measuring 14cm x 38cm (5$\frac{1}{2}$"x15") you will need:
A piece of mahogany-faced plywood remnant 3mm-6mm ($\frac{1}{8}$"-$\frac{1}{4}$") thick measuring 30cm x 38cm (12"x15").

1. Use a compass to draw the outline of the handles as shown. Alternatively, you can use a cup and saucer or plate to do it. The outline does not have to be identical to this, but use it as a guide.

2. Cut the plywood into two identical pieces as shown.

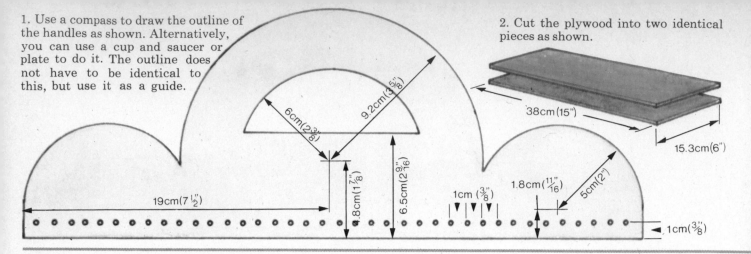

4. To start the inside cut, drill a hole say 6mm (¼") diameter, within the waste area, ie the piece being removed.

drill hole here

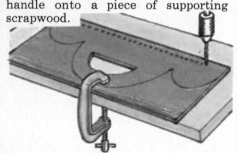

5. Remove the blade from the end pin of the saw. Insert the blade through the hole then fasten the blade back in position and tighten the handle.

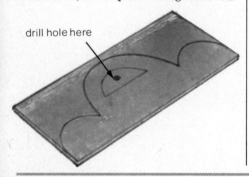

6. Secure the plywood using the C-clamp and saw from the hole to the line and along the line until the hole is completed. It is a bit difficult to saw accurately with such narrow blades—but you can smooth the cut with sandpaper later.

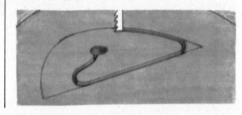

8. Drill 3mm (⅛") diameter holes at each mark using a hand-drill. Avoid splintering the wood as the bit comes out the other side by clamping the handle onto a piece of supporting scrapwood.

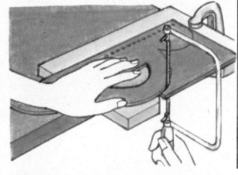

9. Using a sturdy base, and holding the ply firmly, cut along the outline.

10. Sand all the edges and the flat sides first with medium sandpaper to remove all uneven edges—the handle should feel nice and smooth. Then finish with a fine sandpaper.

11. Repeat for the other handle. You can use the first handle to trace the outline to make them identical.
An alternative to drilling all the 3mm (⅛") holes is to cut out a long 2cm (¾") wide slot as shown instead. The bag material will be fastened differently, of course, but just as simply.

12. To finish the handle you can either put on two coats of clear matt polyurethane varnish or you may wish to use an attractive color stain if the plywood is ordinary whitewood.

13. The cloth is attached by folding the top raw edge 12mm (½") and then secured by sewing through the holes.

14. If you have cut a slot instead of drilling holes, pass the material through the slot and stitch it together on the inside below the handle.

Steve Bicknell

3. Trace the outline onto the plywood pieces with a pencil.

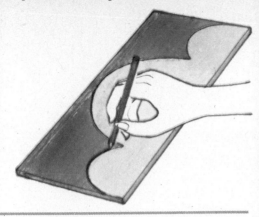

7. Using a nail or a center punch and a hammer, make a small indent at each mark to guide the drill for making the holes used to attach the fabric to the handles.

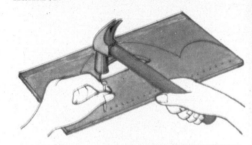

Above: Use wood economically—the animals at the top, cut from one piece of wood, rearranged in the center.

Making your own designs

Now it should be easy to design and make your own handles. Illustrated are two additional handles. One is a simple rectangular design and the other a more stylish Art Deco design. The two rectangular handles measure 23cm x 19cm (9″x7½″). The two Art Deco handles measure 15cm x 33cm (6″x13″). Draw the outline on paper, cut out and trace onto plywood.

Doll's house. You can use an old wooden box to construct a doll's house. The front can be cut out of plywood. Cut out the windows and door, and hinge the door with heavy tape. Paint in the details such as arches over the doors or windows.

Cut-out animals. There are so many other simple objects one can make with the ordinary coping saw; cut-out animals, for example, are fun for children to paint and play with.

You can trace the outlines of animals from books or you can cut out the pictures themselves from magazines and glue them to the plywood before cutting out the shapes.

The legs can be glued to wood blocks to help make the animals stand up. Why not make an entire zoo and print the names on the animals for the children to learn.

You can cut any outlines with a coping saw. Animals are fun and can be painted and labeled for children.

The magic of transfer printing

Color — printing 7

Transfer printing is an amazing process by which a picture or other printed image is actually lifted off a page and put onto another surface. All you need is transfer emulsion, obtainable from most art supply shops, and a nylon brush or plastic sponge to apply it with.

This seascape in oils is really a print transformed on canvas.

Steve Bicknell

552

The process is so simple that any child who can wield a paint brush, tell the time and exercise a little patience can do it. It means that magazine pictures, prints, postcards, old newspaper clippings, even handwritten letters (in ball point pen) can be lifted and transferred onto wood, plastic, glass, metal, leather, paper and cloth.

What happens is that a tough, transparent film is formed by the transfer emulsion which binds printing inks to it, and in this way transfers or lifts the printed image. The film can then be pasted onto another surface.

For this reason photographs cannot be transferred direct. They must have been printed first in a magazine or by some other printing ink process.

In this way you can preserve printed mementos, such as wedding invitations, and transfer them into scrapbooks or use them to decorate other surfaces. A favorite musical score can be put on a paper lampshade, or the printed announcement of a new baby can be applied to a box for a Christmas gift. Photographs from magazines can be made into pillow covers or motifs on screens and curtains. They can also look effective on notebook covers and bookbindings—as can transfers of patterned papers. Window shades, waste paper baskets, trays, boxes and wooden plaques can all be decorated.

Copyright. Many people use transfer printing to make objects for sale, but if you wish to do this consult an authority on copyright laws first. Many pictures have their copyrights retained by the artist or company who produce them and it is therefore illegal for you to sell the image.

Special characteristics

Fabrics. Transfers on fabrics are hand washable, but those items which require frequent washing are less acceptable surfaces than those which do not, so apply them to pillows or curtains rather than jeans or tee shirts. It is also necessary to machine stitch around the edge of the applied image to make sure it stays put.

Glass and ceramic transfers become washable only after a special protective coating (obtainable with the emulsion) is applied.

Textured surfaces. If the surface to which you are applying a transfer print is textured, such as burlap or wood, the texture will be incorporated into the image. For this reason one of the most popular uses of transfer printing is to apply reproductions of Old Master paintings onto canvas. An oil on canvas effect results.

Right: a definite texture like burlap becomes part of the finished picture when transfers are mounted on it.

Above: by transferring the image on a postcard onto wood you can make an icon.

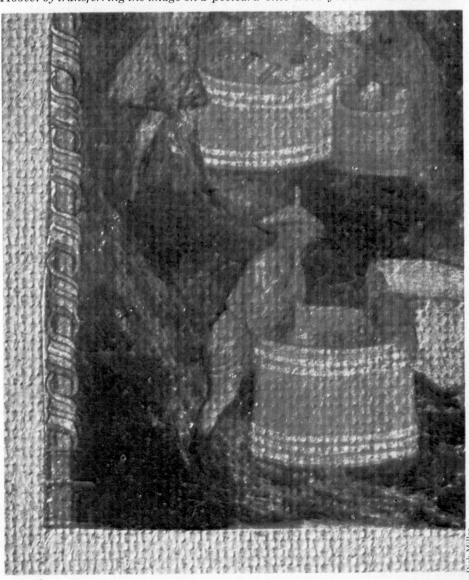

553

1. *To make a transfer print, paint six coats of special emulsion onto printed page, each one in a different direction.*

4. *The image from the page is now contained in the transparent plastic film which can be pasted to other surfaces.*

5. *Paste the image onto a new surface (in this case canvas) by using the transfer emulsion as a glue.*

2. *Soak the coated page in a tray of soapy water for about on hour to loosen the coat of plastic film.*

3. *Peel the page off the plastic film which now contains the image. Remove stubborn bits of paper by rubbing.*

An 'oil on canvas' which began as a photo. (See antiqued effects opposite.)

Dick Miller

How to transfer

Although comparatively easy to master, the transfer process takes several hours to complete because of the drying and soaking required. Therefore it is worth while to do several different transfers at a time.

When selecting the image or lettering for transfer, keep in mind that transfer printing does *not* reproduce the image, it lifts it off the page and the page must be soaked in water to accomplish this and so will be destroyed.

You will need:
Transfer emulsion.

Nylon paint brush or plastic sponge.

Masking or transparent adhesive tape.

Shallow container big enough to soak the image.

Special protective coating, if applying transfer onto glass or ceramics.

Old paper to protect working surface.

If the image you wish to transfer has an unwanted border, keep it for the time being; it will make working easier and can be cut away later.

☐ Tape the picture to a piece of cardboard to hold it steady, or tape brown paper to a work table and then tape the corners of the picture to the brown paper (fig.1).

☐ Using a nylon paint brush or piece of plastic sponge, apply six coats of transfer emulsion to the picture, stroking each coat in a different direction to the one before it. Allow to dry for 15 minutes between coats or until the white color of the emulsion disappears and leaves a glossy, transparent film.

☐ After the final coat, leave the picture for two hours and then put the print into a tub or tray of warm, soapy water and soak for one hour (fig.2).

☐ When you remove the print from the water, place it face down on a hard working surface such as a kitchen table. Then, carefully begin to peel paper from film (fig.3). If it doesn't peel off soak it a little longer. The paper which you peel off will be miraculously blank and you will see the image on the film beneath.

☐ There will always be remaining bits of a thin paper film stuck to the transfer after peeling and it is important that this is removed. So, with your finger begin to rub the surface of the transfer, taking great care not to tear or stretch it.

The remaining paper should rub up in little balls. Different papers do behave differently, however, and some require a great deal of rubbing to remove all the fragments.

Sometimes paper such as newsprint will be broken up in the soaking and the remaining pieces must be rubbed off as it is beyond peeling. Generally speaking, this is the most difficult stage since the transfer film may be torn or

badly stretched by rubbing and some papers need considerable perseverance to remove them.

☐ Rinse the transfer under the tap to get rid of little balls of rolled paper. The image will by now be visible on the back and the front of the film but the front may look clouded. This will disappear when it is dry.

☐ Once dried, check the back again for specks of paper. Any remaining traces can be removed by wetting your finger and rubbing away the spots.

☐ Trim off unwanted borders.

To apply the transfer, you simply use the transfer emulsion as a glue. Coat the back of the film with it and stick it to the surface you wish to decorate, taking care to center it (figs.4, 5).

☐ Start in the center of the image and begin to rub outward to fix the film to the surface and also to remove any air bubbles. Again, take care not to stretch the film. If any bubbles remain, puncture the film with a pin, then press down. Allow to dry.

Glass and ceramic surfaces should be coated with protective fluid to protect the transferred image.

Wood surfaces should be varnished with polyurethane to give protection.

Antiqued finishes can also be made by applying a special crackle varnish designed for use with transfer emulsion. The result is as good as anything of the same type which you buy in shops.

Antiqued effects

By applying a special crackle varnish to the transferred print, and allowing it to dry, hairline cracks will occur into which you then rub artists' raw umber oil paint, from art suppliers. This will produce a cracked finish similar to that produced by age in some varnished surfaces. The crackle varnish is only suitable for surfaces on which the transfer emulsion has been used.

By painting on a special crackling liquid you can make an 'antiqued' look.

Steve Bicknell

Formal flower arrangements

Formal flower arrangements are by definition those that have some pre-determined form or shape to them. Unlike more simply arranged informal flowers they do not rely altogether on the natural beauty of color and texture to make them aesthetically pleasing. They need careful planning to make them successful and the arranger's art shows both in the over-all shape and the positioning of each blossom and piece of foliage. Success depends upon composition and form and the flowers are the raw materials.

Over the years established guidelines have come to be accepted for formal flower arrangements and their rather traditional feeling is best reflected against a similar background.

The more informal atmosphere of most modern homes, and the time and expense involved in making carefully composed arrangements, has meant that formal flowers are now mainly 'special occasion' flowers for decoration at special events such as receptions, club dinners, official gatherings or church services.

Backgrounds

With all forms of flower arranging you must take the background into account because this will determine where the flowers are going to be—the colors, size and shape of arrangement.

If you are arranging flowers for a church or a function in rooms with which you are already familiar, it will be a lot easier for you to select your flowers and plan the size and numbers of arrangements.

If the function is to be in a hotel, or other less familiar accommodation, visit the rooms, make notes on the colors of the walls and curtains and find out about the position of tables and any other furnishings that will affect your choice of flowers.

Always make a point of discussing with caterers the details of the china, table linen, and positioning of tables. White china on a white tablecloth may need vivid floral colors while a pastel cloth will probably look better with softer tones. You must also decide beforehand how many arrangements to make and how big each of them should be.

Flowers for seated dinners should be low enough to allow guests to see each other over them. People sometimes use epergnes, or pedestal-mounted bowls to decorate dinner tables with splendid, cascading arrangements, but these also block the view of dinner guests opposite and this is a mistake no matter how beautiful the flowers.

For such occasions the best arrangements are low, rounded or elongated shapes and these can be made in shallow containers on a base of wire mesh or floral foam.

The number of table arrangements depends on the length of the table and whether candles are used. As a rule, a single center arrangement with flanking candles is sufficient for up to 20 guests; longer tables may have two other smaller arrangements echoing the center one. With U-shaped tables the same theme can be extended to the flanking tables.

Some dinners are arranged with lots of small round tables and in this case identical centerpieces should be used. A tiny bouquet or a slender vase with a single rose or gladiolus is appropriate, although these are not really formal 'arrangements'.

Texture and color rather than shape dominate this D. Hicks' arrangement.

Reception flowers probably give the greatest scope for floral opulence, but here again, background is important.

If there is a mantelpiece you can use it as a natural focal point and place a small arrangement at each end. Chests, pedestals and large side tables are other obvious places and these can take the largest, grandest arrangements. These often present the biggest challenge to the arranger but can also be the most fun to do.

A large entrance hall is usually reserved for the most magnificent arrangement of all and this often takes the form of a large urn filled with a variety of flowers of many colors.

Church flowers can be among the most satisfying of formal arrangements to do because of the enormous amount of space and light which create different effects. When arranging church flowers you must bear in mind the size, style and period of the church itself. Informal bouquets of

Alasdair Ogilvie

wild flowers will look delightful in the small chapel of an ancient or rustic country church but would be totally out of place in a more imposing building. Most church flowers need clear form and shape.

Flowers, particularly those arranged at the chancel steps, must be large and high enough to be visible from the back of the church. It is also better in many cases to have flowers in all shades of one color rather than in contrasting colors so the shape of the arrangement is sufficiently dominant.

Altar flowers present a difficulty because they often have to compete both with altar hangings and stained glass windows. It is sometimes a good idea to choose one of the colors from the stained glass and emphasize this in the flowers. But on the whole, the natural stone or whitewashed walls of many churches make them fine environments for appreciating the beauty of flowers.

Massive formal arrangement by Constance Spry is successfully designed to fill a large space and act as a focal point.

Design ideas

Many ideas are generated by our being responsive to our surroundings, and ideas about flower arrangements are no exception, so make a point of noticing the flowers you see around you. For example, do you find the arrangements you see satisfying, and

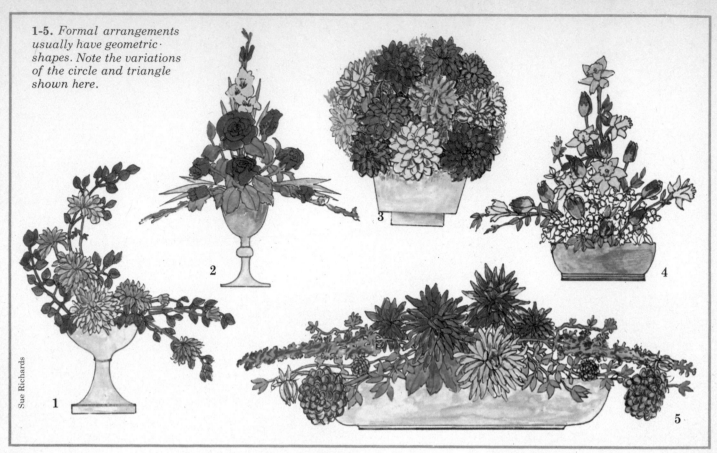

1-5. *Formal arrangements usually have geometric shapes. Note the variations of the circle and triangle shown here.*

Sue Richards

if not, why not? Try to define what displeases or pleases you. Is it the positioning, shape, colors? By making these observations you become more aware of your own personal taste. Noting the colors in household furnishings or clothes can generate ideas about combining colors and tones in floral arrangements, but one of the best ways of getting ideas about creating elegant or luxuriant formal arrangements is to go to the library and look at illustrations of flower paintings, particularly 17th- and 18th century Dutch and French pictures. Once you have begun to appreciate the vivid shape and color through the artist's eye you will be able to look at your own arrangements and then expand your own visual ideas.

Basic equipment
Be sure to have all the equipment ready that you will need—floral scissors, container, wire mesh or floral foam. The various flowers will be put into the container, and through the supporting foam or wire, one at a time according to a basic plan (for more details about the use of basic equipment, Flowers and plants 1, page 472). Remember to give the flowers a good soak up to their necks for several hours before arranging them. Even if they are destined for a single occasion they will look brighter and fresher and often guests like to take flowers home after an event.

Principles of formal arrangements
The outline or shape of formal arrangements is all-important and traditionally the forms used are the circle and the triangle. Figs. 1-5 show variations of these two geometric shapes. Notice that the angles of the triangles differ, making broader or taller arrangements, and the crescent, as a part of the circle, is also used. The three basic steps to follow when attempting any arrangement are really extremely simple.

The outline must be established first by putting in the tall outline material such as delphiniums, gladioli, forsythia, yew, lime (with the leaves stripped off), grasses. Start by placing three pieces to fix the outline points (fig.6) and then add a few more, if you wish, to complete the shape. In formal arrangements all the stems must appear to come from a single point so that the flowers seem to flow outward and upward from a single stem.

Containers can form part of the whole or act as a kind of pedestal supporting the arrangement.

Focal interest is created by the large blooms which form the center of the arrangement and are placed near the middle and as a rule fairly low (fig.7). Important looking blooms such as peonies, rhododendrons, magnolias, roses or tight clusters of berries are ideal, but avoid giving the effect of one central blob of color. Choose flowers which will enhance but not totally dominate the arrangement. Large areas of dark color tend to look heavy and should be kept in the center.

Filling material, for example sweet williams, marguerites or sweet peas—is used to connect the heavier central flowers with the outline (fig.8). Do not be tempted, however, to fill in every single gap you can find. The effect of a flower arrangement can be ruined if it is too tightly packed. Most formal arrangements are designed to be viewed from only one angle and by pointing several stems slightly backward, away from the front, a sense of fullness is created with few flowers.

Choosing flowers. Flowers in all stages, from buds to blossoms, can be used since lighter material must be mixed with the heavy to give grace and elegance. Think about the texture of the flowers and leaves. Leaf texture always affects the weight and balance of an arrangement. A shiny leaf could be used with great effect as a highlight. Do not use strongly textured leaves as outline material, unless they are very pale in color and therefore visually light, or your arrangements will look top heavy.

If possible always have odd numbers of different flowers. Large blooms can usually be bought singly, but many flowers are sold in bunches of even numbers. These can be split up, however, if more than one arrangement is involved.

Alasdair Ogilvie

6. *To build an arrangement like the one above put in tall outline first.*

7. *Large blooms placed near the center give focal interest.*

8. *Use filling material to connect the heavier central flowers and the outline.*

559

Geometric pattern

Johnnie Ryan

A repeated geometric pattern in knitting is decorative and functional.

As well as its decorative function geometric pattern can also play a part in the way in which something works. In knitting, for example, it can be the means of creating a repeated, textured pattern. If used with skill more complicated surfaces can be made with deeper bumps and dents—ribbing, cable stitch and seed stitch.

This kind of pattern lends itself to repetition in the triangles of a star, the hexagons in a patchwork, the rectangles of brick designs, the squares in weaving or in the very long rectangles of stripes.

Surfaces. Geometric pattern can also be applied to surfaces. The design can be printed or painted onto ceramics, paper, cloth and a variety of other materials such as wood, glass and metal.

Here are two experiments which are fun to do and which will help you to see what you can do with basic geometric shapes.

You will need:

Two pieces of white paper or thin cardboard about 0.6m x 0.3m (2'x1').
Scissors.
Paper paste.

Experiment 1

You will also need tissue paper in three contrasting colors.

Cut squares of tissue paper about 23cm x 23cm (9"x9") in all three colors. Cut these again into rectangles, roughly 15cm x 4cm (6"x1½").

Arrange a stripe pattern on the white paper using one color of tissue paper. Leave gaps of up to 7.5cm (3") between the stripes. Stick down the paper (fig.1).

Repeat the process with the second color stripes, placing some stripes in the gaps and partially overlapping the first color (fig.2).

Now look at the pattern.

Add the third color stripes only if you think it will improve matters.

This experiment should produce several unexpected colors where the tissue paper overlaps. Done with thought it can give subtle and varied results. If the original colors are strong they may obscure the paler shades.

Try varying the distance between the stripes and notice the change in the pattern.

Experiment 2

You will also need some brown wrapping paper 45cm x 15cm (1½'x6").

Cut a 15cm x 5cm (6"x2") length of brown paper. Put the short ends together and fold in half, and similarly fold in half again (fig.3). Cut one open end into a simple curve or lop-sided point.

Repeat on another strip the same size but cut out both open ends, making a contrast in size or shape.

With a third piece of paper cut the shape into the folded edges and not the open ends. Straighten out the pieces of paper.

Arrange on the white paper, making some pieces touch and leaving gaps of varying sizes.

You can leave the pattern like this or develop it further by cutting similar strips of colored tissue paper and overlapping as in the first experiment.

There are any number of variations on these designs; try overlapping circles or triangles of various sizes and see what happens.

1

2

3

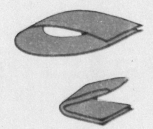

Victoria Drew

1. *Tissue paper in a stripe pattern.* 2. *Arrange a two-color pattern.* 3. *Fold the brown paper twice.*